The Secret

Loves of

the

FOUNDING FATHERS

The Secret Loves of the

FOUNDING FATHERS

The romantic side of George Washington, Thomas Jefferson,

Benjamin Franklin, Gouverneur Morris, Alexander Hamilton

❖◇❖◇❖◇❖◇❖◇❖◇❖◇❖◇❖◇❖◇❖◇❖◇❖◇❖◇❖◇❖◇❖◇❖

Charles Callan Tansill

Professor Emeritus American Diplomatic History

GEORGETOWN UNIVERSITY

ILLUSTRATED

The Devin-Adair Company

New York

1 9 6 4

To my wife, Helen,
an old and ever young sweetheart

1279882

Acknowledgments

Inasmuch as this book grew directly out of my courses in American biography, I owe the inspiration to write it to my students. I am also happy to record my indebtedness to an old friend, Mr. David C. Mearns, chief of the Division of Manuscripts, Library of Congress, who makes research in his division a pleasant and profitable exercise. I owe a similar debt to the able staffs of the New York Public Library, the New York State Library, and the Columbia University Library.

I have received a great deal of inspiration and assistance from my highly esteemed friend, Professor Harry Elmer Barnes, whose work along similar lines brought this topic into sharp focus. My son, Dr. William R. Tansill, helped me in innumerable ways to clarify certain topics and to extend the boundaries of my knowledge of bibliography.

Among some of the friends and scholars who have been of real assistance in the preparation of this book are the following: John Jay Daly, Brigadier Gen. Bonner Fellers, Ralph Townsend, Alice Drake, Rev. Herbert Clancy, S.J., Mrs. Kieran Carroll, Miss Amy Holland, Miss Patricia Paylore, and Verner W. Clapp, most able librarian.

I have dedicated this volume to my wife, Helen C. Tansill, whose constant encouragement and excellent suggestions along with amorous explanations have enabled me to walk bravely along paths with which I have been quite unfamiliar.

C.C.T.

Foreword

My main purpose in writing this little book is to humanize our founding fathers without demeaning them. They were not a cross-section of the American public of their time. Instead, they represented outstanding Americans who had served in a major manner to build the foundations of a unique republic which was to realize the political dreams of great thinkers from Plato to Sir Thomas More. There were many of the so-called founding fathers. I have chosen to write about an illustrious quintet—Washington, Franklin, Jefferson, Gouverneur Morris, and Hamilton—the most eminent member of which was George Washington, whose military genius and superb qualities of leadership brought victory to scanty bands of embattled colonists. In many ways, the American Revolution was George Washington's war.

Jefferson was the inspired penman of the Revolution and the greatest political philosopher America has produced. Franklin was the ablest diplomat of the Revolutionary era; his signal successes in Paris led to French intervention in the war, with the consequent triumph of American arms. Gouverneur Morris' skilled hand put the federal constitution in its final literary form, and in Paris, at the outbreak of the French Revolution, he ably carried on in the tradition of Franklin. Alexander Hamilton, the incomparable financial genius, laid the cornerstone of the American financial edifice that has lasted until the present day.

But these American titans were a very human lot with some very human weaknesses that have been magnified far beyond their proper dimensions. During the American Revolution, British propagandists were busy at their congenial task of smearing the character of George Washington, and they have had many successors who have centered most of their activity around the so-called love affair between George Washington and Sally Fairfax. There is little doubt that George was strongly attracted to Sally, and a few months before his death in 1799 he wrote her a letter in which the note of deep affection is sounded only for her ears. But it was a genuinely Platonic affection which was kept discreetly within bounds, although at times these bounds must have been sorely strained.

With regard to Franklin, most historians and biographers have stressed the practical qualities clearly outlined in the innumerable wise sayings in his yearly almanacs. But Franklin had a personality as fluent as quicksilver, and in some ways he was never quite the same from day to day. The great exception to this fact was his deep-seated and constant patriotism, which dictated a devotion unsurpassed by any of the founding fathers.

Paris seemed to have been the focal point of the amatory adventures some of these outstanding Americans found. When Jefferson became American minister to France after severe trials as governor of Virginia, he found Paris a haven of refuge where the warm friendship of fair women diverted his thoughts from the sad days at Monticello. In Maria Cosway he found a companion whose exceptional beauty and charm opened wide the door of a heart he thought he had securely locked after his dearly loved wife had been interred in distant Virginia. He responded to this reawakening of love by writing love letters that are models of affection, and his famous "Dialogue Between the Head and the Heart" is a classic example of the dilemma of a lover bewildered by the necessity of a quick answer to a sudden call from a demanding love.

The most complex of these founding fathers was Gouverneur Morris, whose *Diary* is an important and very colorful record of the social life in Paris on the eve of the French Revolution. As the American minister to France, Morris had many duties to perform, but his lack of an expert knowledge of written French compelled him to seek assistance. His French dictionary was a seductive French beauty with a most attractive cover and with definitions that usually spelled delight. The quality of his correspondence with the French Foreign Office improved tremendously, and the question arises as to whether private morals should be permitted to interfere with duties of state. At any rate, the Morris chapter has a moral ending. At his ancestral home, Morrisania, Morris ended a bright Christmas Day by marrying his attractive mistress, who provided him with a sturdy son and a wealth of affection which gave him the first real happiness of his very eventful life.

In dealing with Alexander Hamilton, one remembers that the Caribbean spawned him, as it did Napoleon's Empress Josephine, that his hot blood counseled actions which came straight from the heart and not the head. To Mrs. John Adams, Hamilton's "lascivious eyes" indicated the unbridled nature of the man, but to his wife, Betty Schuyler, they were bright beacons of true love.

I first thought of writing this book several decades ago when I was teaching a course in American biography at American University. I became deeply interested in the students' reactions. My main purpose was to instill a feeling of warm patriotism in them, but I noticed that their interest would wane a little if I tried to make our founding fathers into plaster saints. Apparently—and hence the orientation of this book—they wished me to humanize them without demeaning them. Their viewpoint reminded me of a couplet from an old poem by James Whitcomb Riley:

> In fact, to speak in earnest, I believe it adds a charm
> To spice the good a trifle with a little dust of harm.

I noticed that this "little dust of harm," sprinkled during my lectures on the founding fathers, instantly awakened class interest in them and made my course in American biography a shining success. I hope this same "little dust of harm" in the chapters of this book will awaken a similar interest in readers and will make this small volume, like my lectures, a "shining success."

Charles Callan Tansill
Washington, D.C.

Contents

About the Illustrations

Tracking down portraits of the fifteen women involved in the lives of five selected Founding Fathers has not been an easy task. The quest has led from Versailles and the American Embassy in Paris to Colonial Williamsburg, and to museums, societies and individuals all over the country.

We have also tried to present some of the lesser-known likenesses of the Founding Fathers themselves.

Where we have failed to find the best possible portrait, or, as in a few cases, any portrait at all, both author and publisher would be grateful for information so that these may be included in subsequent editions of this book.

In the case of George Washington it was a fairly simple task, reflecting his own uncomplicated character. One could wish for a better portrait of Sally Fairfax than this one, reproduced from the privately issued book, *Sally Cary*, by her descendant, George Miles Cary. However, the John Woolaston portrait of the young Martha Custis Washington (in the possession of G. W. Custis, Esq., Arlington House, D.C.) possesses a charm and sweetness somewhat lacking in later pictures.

The American Philosophical Society in Philadelphia was most helpful in supplying portraits of Ben Franklin, of Deborah Read Rogers and of the "natural" son and grandson. The New York Public Library was cooperative throughout and managed to locate a rare miniature of Madame Helvétius. As for Catherine Ray Greene, we were still trying to reach a descendant at the ancestral Greene farm in Rhode Island, when this book went to press. We did learn of a print of a Madame Brillon portrait, only to find that certain restrictions have been placed upon it by the owners in Paris and we were unable to use it.

Thomas Jefferson presented problems. It seemed logical that his lovely wife Martha Skelton should have been painted by at least one artist in an age when portraits were the rule rather than the exception. But she died in her thirties and it is possible that no likeness exists other than the crayon portrait made by a friend, which we reproduce here, with our thanks to the unknown descendant of the artist, in Mobile, Alabama, into whose possession the portrait has now come. The American Embassy in Paris kindly sent us the print of a miniature of Jefferson's daughter, Martha, said to resemble her mother. The portrait of Mrs. Cosway by herself (from the mezzotint of Valentine Greene) is in the collection of Mr. Edmund B. Martin.

The other ladies in Jefferson's life may have portraits extant and information about them would be welcomed. They are Rebecca Burwell, who became Mrs. Jacqueline Ambler and whom Jefferson referred to as Belinda in his earlier letters, and Betsy Moore, daughter of Benard Moore, who became the wife of William Walker.

The New York Public Library helped in locating portraits of Gouverneur Morris as it did with others in the book. The Bibliothèque Nationale is the source of the Adélaide de Flahaut portrait. The portrait of Nancy Randolph Morris is courtesy of the Frick Art Reference Library. The Talleyrand portrait is in the Musée de Versailles. Alas! Kitty Livingston still eludes us.

And finally Alexander Hamilton and his wife are shown without an attempt having been made to find a portrait of the notorious Mrs. Reynolds, who probably needed a Hogarth to do her justice.

Portraits

The Secret

Loves of

the

FOUNDING FATHERS

one

George Washington
[1732-1799]

THE FLAMES OF YOUTH

There are several hundred biographies of George Washington, and they display him in myriad different lights. In some of them he is extravagantly praised, and in the famous biography by Parson Weems there is more myth than fact. But the Parson did have the knack of putting color into his narrative, and it had great influence upon several generations of Americans. Some biographers have endeavored to debunk Washington, but they found it difficult to minimize the epic exploits of a man whose vision and courage brought a relatively small number of poorly prepared colonists to victory through seven long years of desperate warfare. In many ways it was certainly General Washington's war.

His astounding success was so overwhelming that the man and the image became completely fused, and few biographers have dared to intimate that George was a very human person and not the chill, inhuman model depicted in thousands of adoring pages. In 1877, when some correspondence of Sally Fairfax's was discovered and printed, certain letters addressed to her by George Washington sounded a note of love so strong and clear that the old image of Washington had to be discarded. It was obvious that in colonial days Washington's eyes had kindled at the sight of Sally.

She lived at Belvoir, close to Mount Vernon, and propinquity has long been an important factor in equations of the heart. She was the lovely wife of Washington's most intimate friend, George William Fairfax. It is true that the walls of matrimony have never been able to prevent the roving eyes of ardent men from paying court to beautiful women who keep some small corner of their hearts reserved for men other than their husbands. There is no doubt that at times Washington expressed his love for Sally Fairfax in a rush of words that pushed aside all barriers of restraint; but one also remembers that the poet Dante wrote immortal sonnets to Beatrice, another man's wife, and the world has long rejoiced that her beauty inspired a sonnet cycle of imperishable poems.

Love did inspire Washington sometimes to write poems to girls he thought he loved, but no one has ever asserted that they resemble the sonnets of Dante. Doubtless Washington realized his limitations in this regard, and it is certain that he never addressed any poems to Sally Fairfax. He did, however, write letters to her in which the bright edge of love is evident through the dark torrent of words that his impetuous pen cast onto the paper.

Washington was never backward about acknowledging the hold that strong emotions had upon him. A few years before his death he wrote this significant letter:

Love is said to be an involuntary passion, and it is, there-fore, contended that it cannot be resisted. This is true in part only, for like all things else, when nourished and sup-plied plentifully with aliment, it is rapid in its progress; but let these be withdrawn and it may be stifled in its birth or much stinted in its growth. For example, a woman . . . all beautiful and accomplished will, while her hand and heart are undisposed of, turn the heads and set the circle in which she moves on fire. Let her marry, and what is the consequence? The madness *ceases* and all is quiet again. Why? Not because there is any diminution in the charms of the lady, but because there is an end of hope. Hence it follows, that love may and therefore ought to be under the guidance of reason, for although we cannot avoid first impressions, we may assuredly place them under guard.[1]

At sixty-six, when the fires of life were beginning to burn low, he could write fluently about the course of conduct a young man should follow with reference to a charming young lady who had married another man—he should by all means control his passion for a married woman. But this was a counsel of perfection that Washington himself did not follow with regard to Sally Fairfax. He could not avoid his "first impressions" of her beauty, and the "mad-ness" in his blood continued unabated for a decade.

But before his warm affection for Sally Fairfax became a

[1] Paul L. Ford, *The True George Washington* (Philadelphia, 1896), p. 84.

fixation, he indulged in some lesser currency of the heart
in several affairs with girls of the neighborhood. His interest in a certain "Low Land Beauty" is disclosed in a letter
to one of his friends:

Dear Friend Robin:

My place of Residence is at present at His Lordships
where I might, was my heart disengag'd, pass my time
very pleasantly as theres a very agreeable Young Lady
lives in the same house (Colo George Fairfax's Wife's
Sister) but as thats only adding Fuel to fire it makes me
the more uneasy for by often and unavoidably being in
Company with her revives my former Passion for your
Low Land Beauty whereas was I to live more retired
from young Women I might in some measure eliviate my
sorrows by burying that chast and troublesome Passion in
the grave of oblivion or eternall forgetfulness for as I am
very well assured thats the only antidote or remedy that
I shall be releived by or only recess that can administer
any cure or help to me as I am well convinced was I ever
to attempt anything I should only get a denial which
would be only adding grief to uneasiness.[2]

For many years biographers of Washington have tried to
identify this "Low Land Beauty." Mary Bland of West-
moreland has been suggested as the girl about whom he
writes, but some historians have inclined to the belief that
Lucy Grymes was the beauty who had awakened in
Washington's heart that "chast and troublesome Passion"
which he wished to bury "in the grave of oblivion." In
time Lucy married Henry Lee of Stratford, and became
the mother and grandmother of famous Virginians. Among

[2] George Washington, *Writings*, ed. W. C. Ford (New York, 1889-
1893, 14 vols.), I, 7.

her children was Lighthorse Harry Lee, a distinguished
cavalry officer in the Revolution and a favorite of Washington. She had a grandson even more famous—Robert
E. Lee.[3] This grandson married Mary Ann Custis, the
daughter of Martha Custis' grandson George Washington
Parke Custis, whom Washington had adopted as his own
son. In this way, Lucy Grymes and George had ties that
were forever famous.

Another letter from Washington, at an early date, was
addressed to

Dear Sally:

This comes to Fredericksburg fair in hopes of meeting
with a speedy Passage to you if your not there which hope
youl get shortly altho I am almost discouraged from writing to you as this is my fourth to you since I receiv'd any
from yourself. I hope youl not make the Old Proverb good
out of sight out of Mind as its one of the greatest Pleasures
I can yet foresee of having in Fairfax in often hearing from
you hope you'l not deny it me.[4]

One cannot greatly blame Sally for not answering letters so confused and juvenile. And it would seem that
Washington's heart was not too badly affected by this
feminine indifference: according to rumor, his attention
was soon attracted by Mary Cary when she came to live
at Belvoir with her sister Sally. Mary was only fourteen at

[3] Rupert Hughes, *George Washington, the Human Being and the
Hero, 1732-1762* (New York, 1926-1929, 2 vols.), I, 53; Burton J. Hendrick, *The Lees of Virginia* (Boston, 1935), pp. 136, 173, 346, 391, 405-
438.
[4] George Washington, *Writings, 1745-1799*, ed. John C. Fitzpatrick
(Washington, D. C., 1931-1944, 39 vols.), I, 16-17.

that time, but George found her a "very agreeable Young Lady." He was a mere stripling, just approaching his seventeenth birthday, and as his correspondence clearly shows, he was a diamond in the rough who required love as a lapidary to smooth him over so that his real personality could shine through. Mary had only a small part in this buffing process.

Colonel William Fairfax, George's father and the head of the Belvoir household, was a man of wide experience. He had served in both the Royal Army and Navy, and had settled in Virginia for the prime purpose of managing the vast estate of his cousin Lord Fairfax. He was a man of wealth and distinction. His hospitable home was "ever a favorite resort of officers of the army and navy, and persons of note from abroad would scarcely visit Virginia without letters to the Fairfaxes." [5]

George's elder half-brother Lawrence married Colonel Fairfax's daughter Anne, thus ensuring the support of one of the most respected gentlemen in Virginia. When Lawrence invited George to make his home at Mount Vernon, close by Belvoir, he helped in a significant manner to fashion his entire career. George was now thrown into "intimate relations with the elegant society of Belvoir. Here his manners were patterned after the best models, his sentiments refined and his views enlarged by contact with clever men and women of a superior class." [6]

The refining influences of Belvoir took some time to sink in, and for a brief period George was left free to indulge his fondness for what he called poetry. One poem was an acrostic probably written for Frances Alexander, who lived on a plantation near Mount Vernon:

[5] Wilson M. Cary, *Sally Cary* (New York, 1916), pp. 24-25.
[6] *Ibid.*, pp. 26-27.

From your bright sparkling Eyes, I was undone;
Rays, you have more transparent than the sun,
Amidst its glory in the rising Day,
None can you equal in your bright array;
Constant in your calm and unspotted Mind;
Equal to all, but will to none prove kind,
So Knowing, seldom one so Young, you'l Find
Ah! woe's to me, that I should love and conceal,
Long have I wish'd, but never dare reveal,
Even though severly Loves Pains I feel;
Xerxes that great, was't free from Cupid's Dart,
And all the greatest Heroes, felt the smart.[7]

Apparently this poetic effort did not open the door of Frances' heart, so George tried his hand at another poem. It might have turned the trick if he could have recited it in some fragrant bower on a soft June night when a full moon might have induced in the girl a mood of pleasant lunacy.

Oh Ye Gods why should my Poor Resistless Heart
Stand to oppose thy might and Power
At Last surrender to cupid's feather'd Dart
And now lays Bleeding every Hour
For her that's Pityless of my grief and Woes
And will not on me Pity take
He sleep amongst my most inveterate Foes
And with gladness never wish to wake
In deluding sleepings let my Eyelids close
That in an enraptured Dream I may
In a soft lulling sleep and gentle repose
Possess those joys denied by Day.[8]

[7] Douglas S. Freeman, *George Washington* (New York, 1948, 7 vols.), I, 260.

[8] Quoted in Ford, *op. cit.*, p. 87.

The leisure that permitted the writing of sonnets was rudely interrupted in March, 1748, by a commission from Lord Fairfax to survey some of his vast holdings in the Northern Neck of Virginia and in the Shenandoah Valley. He was eager to have these lands surveyed correctly and parceled out in modest farms and manor estates. The party was in the charge of George Fairfax, whose father had supplemented Washington's knowledge of the profession of surveying. For wages George was to receive an amount that varied from a doubloon a day to 6 pistoles. It is estimated that this salary would now be reckoned at from "twenty to fifty dollars a week." [9] His income was increased by the efforts of Lord Fairfax, who secured for him the post of public surveyor at a salary of £100 per year.

This steady income was important for George, who had begun to take more interest in his personal appearance. At seventeen, when he was about to take a trip, his wardrobe consisted of nine shirts, six linen waistcoats, a cloth waistcoat, six neckbands, four neck cloths, and seven caps. Why he would need seven caps I do not know. His further interest in girls was indicated by his attendance at a dancing school. As a mentor in social graces and sartorial elegance, Lawrence was always at hand for sage advice.

The brief surveying trip in the spring of 1748 opened Washington's eyes to the importance of acquiring lands across the mountains. His interest in landowning grew rapidly when his half-brothers, Lawrence and Augustine, became members of the Ohio Company. The King of England had granted half a million acres to the company on the condition that it build and maintain a fort on the lands, which were also claimed by the French. Washing-

[9] Hughes, *op. cit.*, I, 40.

ton was later sent by Governor Dinwiddie to warn French intruders away from this transmountain country. He regarded this commission as largely a family affair. The French were trespassing upon territory in which his half-brothers had a financial interest, and with the Washingtons family ties were close.

WASHINGTON MEETS SALLY FAIRFAX

But before George Washington became a soldier, he had an experience that molded his entire career: he met and fell deeply in love with Sally Cary Fairfax, who had married Washington's close friend George in December, 1748. The effect of Washington's first meeting with Sally was electric, and the spark that was kindled was never extinguished. According to Wilson M. Cary, at Belvoir Washington came under the spell "of the most charming woman he had ever met, and from the subtle influence of whose magnetism the strongest efforts of his remarkable will seem to have been powerless to disenthrall him." [10]

Mr. Cary is not the only historian of colonial Virginia who believed that Washington could never throw off the spell of Sally Fairfax. Mrs. Sally Nelson Robins, once the national historian of the Colonial Dames of America, wrote this colorful paragraph about the relations between Washington and Sally Fairfax:

The flame smouldered on and on, and perhaps was never extinguished even to the day of Washington's death. After Sally married Fairfax, Washington was frequently at

[10] Cary, *op. cit.*, p. 27.

Belvoir and Mrs. Fairfax became his patron and instructress in the fine arts of courtesy and good breeding, while her brain, in its strength and flowering, matched his. . . . She enmeshed him with her charm and beauty, and while his affection for her, as he has it, was chaste, it was, probably, no less troublesome. Again, his congenital and marvelous restraint kept him absolutely from the semblance of mischief. I consider his early romances but zephyrs to this one crimson whirlwind passion of his life.[11]

As one looks at the attractive portrait of Sally painted in an orchard at Belvoir, it is easy to understand the impact of her beauty upon Washington. Her eyes, large and bright, were an invitation to happiness, while her mouth, with its full lower lip, gave an unmistakable hint that in any dialogue between the head and the heart, the heart would have a lot to say. To Washington her smile seemed like dawn gilding the distant hills of Maryland far across the broad Potomac. It is obvious that she would have been most unhappy in an ordinary convent, although some recent accounts insist that Eloise, the ardent abbess of an interesting convent in medieval France, looked back most fondly and unashamedly upon that violet-colored moment when Abelard cast restraint to some wild wind and repeated with Eloise the drama of Adam and Eve in the Garden of Eden.

There is no clear evidence that Washington and Sally Fairfax had even a brief dalliance in the Garden of Eden, but Rupert Hughes, in his *Life of George Washington*, inclines to the view that they at least looked over the garden wall. In discussing this bright romance, he remarks:

[11] Sally Nelson Robins, *Love Stories of Famous Virginians* (Richmond, 1925), p. 21.

Eventually, Sally must have fallen pretty deeply into the romance, unless his letters are not to be believed. In any case, they dwelt together in close communion. . . . So Sally and George were on terms of intimacy. And what in timacy meant in some of those country houses on festive occasions can hardly be imagined now.[12]

Fun-making in colonial Virginia was a little boisterous and perhaps a little imprudent, as the diary of Lucinda Lee in 1782 amply discloses:

October 11th. Hannah and myself were going to take a long walk this evening but were prevented by two horred Mortals, Mr. Pinkard and Mr. C. Washington, who seized me and kissed me a dozen times in spite of all the resistance I could make. They really think, now they are married, they are prevaliged to do any things.

[*27th.*]   When we got here we found the House pretty full. Nancy was here. . . . About sunset, Nancy, Milly, and myself took a walk in the Garden. . . . We were mighty busy cutting thistles to try our sweethearts, when Mr. C. Washington caught us; and you can't conceive how he plagued us—chased us all over the Garden, and was quite impertinent.

I must tell you of our frolic after we went in our room. We took it into our heads to want to eat; we had a large dish of bacon and beef; after that a bowl of Sago cream; and after that, an apple pye. While we were eating the apple pye in bed—God bless you, making a great noise— in came Mr. Washington dressed in Hannah's short gown and petticoat, and seazed me and kissed me twenty times, in spite of all the resistance I could make.[13]

---

12 Hughes, *op. cit.*, I, 185.
13 Lucinda Lee Dalrymple, *A Journal of a Young Lady of Virginia, 1782* (Baltimore, 1871).

This journal does not deal with any skylarking of *George* Washington, but it is likely that during these country festivities he was as active as any of his cousins. As Rupert Hughes once more remarks:

> Since there was always dancing going on, George and Sally must have danced together often and long; and for grace and insatiable ardor in the dance, Washington was famous. . . . Those who are forced to admit that Washington loved to dance, often blandly assume that he never indulged in anything less stately than the minuet, or held a lady closer than her uplifted finger-tips. But the Virginians had their country dances, too, and jigs and kissing dances, and as much hugging went on then as now. . . . Horror was expressed even then as of late, at the custom of leaving off corsets for the dance. . . . The rhapsody of the dance till dawn never wearied him.[14]

Washington knew Sally Fairfax well enough to depend upon her to direct her seamstress, who was making a fine ruffled shirt for him:

Dear Madam:

John informs me that you told him Miss Nancy was to be at your House in a day or two: and that you would, if I sent my Linnen over, give it to Miss Nancy to make:—I shall readily embrace the oppertunity of doing this, tho' I am at the same time, sorry to give you the trouble about the directing of the making.

I have sent a piece of Irish Linnen, a piece of Cambrick and a shirt to measure by. The Shirt Fits tolerably well, yet, I would have the others made with somewhat narrower Wrist bands: Ruffles deeper by half an Inch: and

[14] Hughes, *op. cit.*, I, 190-191.

the Collars by three quarters of an Inch, which is in other respects of proper bigness. If Miss Nancy will do me the favour to get thread and buttons suitable it will oblige me much. I have really forget to procure them myself. Please to make my Compts. to Miss Fairfax and Miss West when you see her.[15]

In the fall of 1751, Washington accompanied Lawrence on a trip to the island of Barbados in the hope that the warmer climate would be of benefit to his half-brother's health. Tuberculosis had marked Lawrence as a victim, and the medical science of that day had no prescription for treatment other than a mild climate. A brief stay on the island, from November, 1751, to June, 1752, proved of little aid to Lawrence's health; he died at Mount Vernon on July 26, 1752.

In the spring of 1752, some months before Lawrence's death, George became interested in Betsy Fauntleroy, who lived in Richmond County. Betsy was only in her sixteenth year and had little of the sophistication of Sally Fairfax. She showed scant enthusiasm for George's advances, and he promptly developed an attack of pleurisy which called a sudden halt in his plans. May was well advanced before he felt able to write her a letter under cover of one to her father, William Fauntleroy:

Sir:

I should have been down long before this, but my business in Frederick detained me somewhat longer than I expected, and immediately on my return from thence I was taken with a violent pleurise, which has reduced me

15 Quoted in Eugene E. Prussing, *George Washington in Love and Otherwise* (Chicago, 1924), pp. 8-9.

very low; but purpose, as soon as I recover my strength, to wait on Miss Betsy, in hopes of a revocation of the former cruel sentence, and see if I can meet with any alteration in my favor. I have enclosed a letter to her, which should be much obliged to you for the delivery of it. I have nothing to add but my best respects to your good lady and family.[16]

George's tactic of sending her a letter under cover of one to her father apparently displeased Betsy, who concluded that faint heart should never win fair lady. She first married Bowler Cocke, and after his death wed Thomas Adams, who subsequently became a member of the Continental Congress.

In this same year of 1752, Sally Fairfax's sister Mary Cary married Edward Ambler, and thus the girls whose names had been connected with Washington entered into the state of matrimony with men whose social position in Virginia had been superior to his. Indeed, Rupert Hughes makes the following comment about Edward Ambler's courtship of Mary Cary: "In the face of such competition, Washington was an illiterate boor." [17] This statement is, of course, wide of the mark. Washington was not illiterate, although his poems and letters of this period show that he was an inveterate rebel against the king's English. But he was never a boor, and surely his record of amatory failures was partly due to the fact that the girl he really loved was forever beyond his reach.

Perhaps he would do better as a soldier. In this regard his opportunity was at hand. When Lawrence Washington died in July, 1752, his office as adjutant of the colony

---

[16] Washington, *Writings,* ed. Fitzpatrick, I, 22.
[17] Hughes, *op. cit.,* I, 66.

became vacant. George at once pressed his claim to that post upon Governor Dinwiddie despite the fact that he had never seen a day's service as a soldier. The duties of adjutant were carefully prescribed: he was to instruct "the officers and soldiers in the use and exercise of their arms, in bringing the militia to a more regular discipline, and fitting it for service, besides polishing and improving the meaner people." [18]

George's claim was strongly supported by Lord Fairfax, whose influence was so potent that a compromise was effected. Virginia was now divided into four districts, each of which was to have an adjutant as its chief military officer. George was given the southern district, which extended from Princess Anne County to the western fringe of settlement.

Thus, before he was twenty-one years of age, Washington had been given an important military office with the rank of major. He was also allowed pay at the rate of £100 per annum; and his office as county surveyor granted him a similar amount. It was not long before he had bought 2000 acres of choice land in the Shenandoah Valley. These, together with previous purchases and the land he had inherited, brought his landholdings to a total of 4291 acres of unencumbered property, and in this way he moved into the class of large proprietors. Socially, "he was capable of entering the best of colonial society without embarrassment." [19]

Washington learned that the militia would be called to service in September, 1753, and so he set himself to many months of careful study of military tactics and the elements of military operations. French armed forces had

[18] Freeman, *op. cit.*, I, 268.
[19] *Ibid.*, I, 269.

moved into the Ohio Valley, and were preparing actively
to contest control over that area with the English. Because
Governor Dinwiddie as well as the Washingtons had financial interests in the Ohio Company, it was inevitable
that prompt efforts would be made to warn French intruders to keep off British soil. George Washington requested that he be chosen to deliver this warning, and
Governor Dinwiddie readily acceded.

Washington's hurried trip to the French fort was carried
out in the face of such incredible hardships that the brief
journal of his trip became a Virginia saga of epic adventure and spread his fame far and wide throughout the
colony.[20] But some months later, in July, 1754, he suffered
defeat at Fort Necessity, and this bit of adversity changed
the picture considerably. After a quarrel with Governor
Dinwiddie over the question of his rank, he resigned his
commission as adjutant. But with the French and Indian
War in full swing he could not remain out of the military
service for long. When General Edward Braddock assumed command of all the British military forces that were
preparing to move against the French invaders of the Ohio
Valley in February, 1755, Washington's hurt feelings
were assuaged by an offer of a position on Braddock's staff
with the honorary rank of colonel.

In the late spring of 1755 Washington was quartered
briefly at Fort Cumberland, from which on May 14 he
wrote a brief letter to Sally Fairfax:

Dear Madam:

I have at last with great pains and difficulty discovered
the reason why Mrs. Wardrope is a greater favorite of Genl.
Braddock than Mrs. F——x, and met with more respect at

[20] Washington, *Writings,* ed. Fitzpatrick, I, 22-30.

the review in Alexandria. The cause I shall communicate, after having rallied you upon neglecting the means which produced the effect. And what do you think they were? Why, nothing less, I assure you, than a present of delicious cake and potted wood-cocks: Which so affected the palate as to leave a deep impression upon the hearts of *all* who tasted of them. How, then, could the General do otherwise than admire, not only the *charms*, but the politeness, of this lady!

We have a *favourable* prospect of halting here three weeks or a month longer, for wagons, horses and forage; it is easy to conceive, therefore, that my situation will not be *very pleasant* and agreeable, when I dreaded this (before I came out) more than all the other incidents which might happen during the campaign.[21]

Shortly after writing this letter, George was taken seriously ill with an attack of dysentery, and did not rejoin Braddock until July 8. Before coming down with this attack of camp fever, George wrote Sally a short letter endeavoring to find out his real score in the game of hearts he had been playing with her for seven long years:

Dear Madam:

When I had the happiness to see you last you express'd an inclination to be inform'd of my safe arrival in Camp with the Charge that was entrusted to my care. But at the same time desir'd it might be communicated in a Letter to somebody of your acquaintance. This I took as a gentle rebuke and a polite manner of forbidding my corresponding with you: and [I] conceive this opinion is not illy founded when I reflect that I have hitherto found it impracticable to engage one moment of your attention. If I am right in this, I hope you will excuse the present presumption and lay the imputation to elateness at my suc-

21 Quoted in Prussing, *op. cit.*, pp. 9-10.

cessful arrival. If, on the contrary, these are fearful appre-
hensions only, how easy is it to remove my suspicions,
enliven my spirits, and make me happier than the day is
long, by honouring me with a corrispondance which you
did once partly promise me to do.[22]

This letter was merely a light tap on the door of her
heart. If she opened it in the slightest degree he was ready
to whisper a message that had rested on the tip of his
tongue since that first night at Belvoir. Was her insistence
upon an indirect correspondence an indication that she
did not want her husband to become aware of the tones
of warm affection his letters scarcely concealed? Was she
now ready to stop being coy and give him a slight sign that
he could play Adam to her Eve?

George did not have much time to nurse these pleasant
thoughts. On July 9, Braddock's army suffered a disastrous
defeat, and the general was mortally wounded. One bright
spot in the day of terror was Washington's courageous de-
portment. Two horses were shot from under him and his
clothes were pierced by bullets in several places. He was
a luminous example of what colonial officers could do in
times of dire emergency, and his name became a household word in Virginia. When he returned to Mount Vernon he received a note from Sally Fairfax, signed as a
joint letter by three ladies but written in Sally's clear hand:

Dear Sir:

After thanking Heaven for your safe return I must accus
you of great unkindness in refusing us the pleasure of seeing you this night. I do assure you nothing but our being
satisfied that our Company would be disagreeable should
prevent us from trying if our Legs would not carry us to

[22] Quoted in Cary, *op. cit.*, pp. 21-22.

Mount Vernon this night, but if you will not come to us tomorrow Morning very early we shall be at Mount Vernon.[23]

> S. FAIRFAX
> ANN SPEARING
> ELIZTH DENT.

Sally was still being coy, and if her solicitude for George's health ever broke through the formal barriers of a joint letter, the evidence is not available. Let us hope that the glamour that attends a hero home from the wars held enough warmth to melt the ice that surrounded her heart. But she had little time to woo his mind away from the wars. On August 14, Governor Dinwiddie sent him a commission as "Colonel of the Virg'a Regim't and Com'd'r-in-Chief of all the Forces now rais'd and to be rais'd for the Defence of y's H. M'y's Colony." And he was charged "with full Power and Authority to act defensively and Offensively, as You shall think for the good and Welfare of the Service." [24]

This was a signal honor for a youth of twenty-four years, and George lost no time in immediately accepting the commission. But he was still deeply concerned about the discrimination between royal and colonial military commissions, and asked Governor Dinwiddie to grant him permission to visit Governor Shirley of Massachusetts, who had been made commander in chief of all military forces in America. Dinwiddie graciously granted George's request, and he made his preparations to embark on his first trip through the populous seaboard colonies. He went

[23] Quoted in Stanislaus M. Hamilton, ed., *Letters to Washington and Accompanying Papers* (Boston, 1898, 2 vols.), I, 73.

[24] Washington, *Writings,* ed. Fitzpatrick, I, 161.

north trailing clouds of glory. His outfit was resplendent: he paid £12/10 "for a Hatt," his tailor's bill was £95/7, and for "Silver Lace" he expended the extravagant sum of nearly £95. There is little doubt that he believed that clothes help to make the man.

One of George's biographers makes much of his handsome appearance and his supposed way with women:

> Young, handsome, with the second fortune in the province, and family as good as any, . . . with the first military reputation among the soldiers Virginia's war against the French and Indians had trained, no man in Virginia would naturally be received by the matrons and maids who clustered at the country houses along the Potomac . . . with more cordial welcome than Colonel Washington. What wonder, then, that he fell in love with every pretty girl and told her so, in his visitings among his neighbors, and on official journeys to and from Williamsburgh. . . . Washington was man all over—a man with strong appetites, fierce temper, positive, belligerent, and aggressive.[25]

If George had been half so overwhelming as this lurid description has him, he would have settled the Sally Fairfax situation, for better or worse, in a matter of months instead of years. But the old tradition that he was an aggressive lover has lingered on, and Woodrow Wilson, also a Virginian and a President, makes these colorful comments about George:

> No young Virginian could live twenty-six years amidst fair women in that hale and sociable colony without be-

[25] Bradley T. Johnson, *General Washington* (New Hampshire, 1895), pp. 68-69.

ing touched again and again by the quick passion; and this man had the blood of a lover beyond his fellows. Despite the shyness of a raw lad who lived much in the open, he had relished the company of lively women from the first, meeting their gay sallies sometimes with a look from his frank blue eyes that revealed more than he knew.[26]

In this interesting description, Woodrow Wilson was disclosing a lot more of his own personality than of George's, but that is another story. In the meantime we shall speed George on his trip to see Governor Shirley of Massachusetts. In New York City he stayed with an old Virginia friend, Beverly Robinson, son of the speaker of the Virginia House of Burgesses. Robinson had married Susanna Philipse, heiress to a large fortune. Susanna had a sister Mary, who was far prettier than a rich girl had to be. Washington was informed that her estate was estimated at more than 50,000 acres. But the fly in this amorous ointment was that Mary Philipse already had a devoted suitor, who turned out to be none other than Captain Roger Morris, a comrade at arms with Washington on the day of Braddock's defeat. Once more Washington was on the losing side of a love triangle, but there was tall talk if he had really had the "blood of a lover beyond his fellows" the story might have been different. Had his latent affection for Sally Fairfax kept him from pressing his suit with the required ardor?

After this unsuccessful bout with Cupid in New York, George moved on to Boston. Governor Shirley was quite helpful. He issued an order that Captain Dagworthy of Maryland, who had been a large thorn in Washington's

[26] Woodrow Wilson, *George Washington* (New York, 1903), p. 101.

side at Fort Cumberland, should be subordinate to the famous Virginian: "In case it should happen, that Colonel Washington and Captain Dagworthy should join at Fort Cumberland, it is my order that Colonel Washington shall take command." [27]

Command along the frontier was a thankless task at best. Marauding bands of French and Indians maintained the Blue Ridge Mountains as the western boundary of Virginia, and lack of funds and supplies made it difficult for George to keep his regiment in shape for actual combat. Moreover, life in the frontier forts was so uncomfortable and amusements so few that stories circulated all over Virginia about the drunkenness and immorality that were rife in the ranks of Washington's regiment. The Earl of Loudoun, commander in chief of all the military forces in the colonies, realized long before Rudyard Kipling that single men in barracks don't grow into plaster saints, and did not spend much time looking for halos. Washington was informed that the Earl, after reading the evidence, seemed "very much pleased with the accounts you have given him." [28]

But there were no further major expeditions against French forts by way of the historic Virginia highway to the Ohio Valley, and Washington's role became quite secondary. To add to his discomfort, he was relieved of the management of Indian affairs along the Virginia frontier, and was placed in subordination to Colonel Stanwix, whom Loudoun put in charge of all the troops from Pennsylvania, Maryland, and Virginia. Constant friction and worry about conditions along the fringe of settlement took

[27] William Shirley, *Correspondence*, ed. Charles H. Lincoln (New York, 1912, 2 vols.), II, 412.
[28] Quoted in Hughes, *op. cit.*, I, 324.

a severe toll on Washington's health and brought about another protracted case of dysentery. In the spring of 1758 he had a foreboding that "death was near," so he decided to consult a doctor at Williamsburg. While there he met a comely and wealthy widow, Martha Dandridge Custis, and his health immediately improved.

WASHINGTON MEETS MARTHA CUSTIS

Martha Dandridge had married Daniel Parke Custis in 1749, and lived in the famous Six Chimney House in Williamsburg. Custis was not a man of rugged health, and his children were sickly. A daughter, Martha, called by her nickname Patsy, was a victim of fits and died in her childhood. The son, John Parke Custis, was reasonably healthy but lacked initiative and ambition. Of Martha herself, Paul L. Ford makes the following critical comment: "Very little is known of his wife, beyond the facts that she was petite, over-fond, hot tempered, obstinate, and a poor speller. In 1778 she was described as 'a sociable, pretty kind of woman,' and she seems to have been but little more." [29]

In one of his moods of jealousy of Washington, John Adams asked a question which many persons thought was not worthy of an answer: "Would Washington have ever been commander of the revolutionary army or President of the United States if he had not married the rich widow of Mr. Custis?" Adams conveniently overlooked the fact that Washington's military fame in 1775 had been achieved before his marriage and was not furthered by any of the wealth of Mrs. Custis. It is true, of course, that

[29] Ford, *op. cit.*, p. 93.

Mrs. Custis possessed a large fortune. Her third of the Custis property amounted to some 15,000 acres of valuable land, part of which adjoined Williamsburg. In addition she owned several lots in the city and had eight or ten thousand pounds under bond, along with several hundred negroes. All together, after the death of Patsy Custis in 1773, Martha must have had an estate worth close to £30,000. She was indeed a widow with a broad golden smile.[30]

But in wooing Martha Custis, George was saying farewell to romance and closing forever the door upon the great love of his life. He had deeply loved Sally Fairfax for a decade, but she had repulsed all his efforts, however faint, to make their relationship a little more meaningful than just friendship. In the early years of their acquaintance she had seemed like some insubstantial being who represented inspiration rather than desire. But as the years lengthened and his needs increased, he realized that he must have a responsive woman and not merely a friend who wished to remain only that. If Sally ever prided herself on having a conscience that kept her true to her husband, it may well have been merely a case of cold feet.

It has been said that Washington was attracted to Martha Custis partly because of her close resemblance to Mary Cary, Sally's sister. If this hypothesis is correct, George may have thought that in marrying Martha he would always have close to him a reminder of the girl he really loved. Certainly there was no resemblance between Sally Fairfax and Martha Custis. Sally was tall and intellectual, with an intriguing hint of warm desire beneath a protective layer of repression. Martha was petite, sexually attractive, and poorly educated. Her spelling was

[30] *Ibid.*, pp. 94-95.

atrocious and her vocabulary limited; she had trouble even with simple correspondence. Sally was a great lady, cool and elusive; Martha was pure housewife and obvious. But Washington was apparently weary of chasing a will-o'-the-wisp and wanted a real woman, not a wraith.

In the case of Mrs. Custis it is evident that she needed an able manager for her large estate. Her lawyer had advised her to "employ a trusty steward, and, as the estate is large and very extensive . . . you had better not engage any but a very able man." [31] She had found her man.

But her man had to hurry back to the army, where he was busily engaged at Winchester trying to raise two regiments. He was able, however, to write her a brief note:

July 20, 1758

We have begun our march to the Ohio. A courier is starting for Williamsburg, and I embrace the opportunity to send a few words to one whose life is now inseparable from mine. Since that happy hour when we made our pledges to each other, my thoughts have been continually going to you as another Self. That an all-powerful Providence may keep us both in safety is the prayer of your ever faithful and affectionate friend.[32]

This warm letter to Mrs. Custis had hardly reached Williamsburg when George received a letter from Sally Fairfax. There is no copy of her letter in existence, and we can only judge of its contents by the answering letter George wrote to her in the second week of September. Apparently she had playfully taunted him with her knowl-

[31] Quoted in Anne H. Wharton, *Martha Washington* (New York, 1897), pp. 25-36.
[32] Washington, *Writings,* ed. Fitzpatrick, II, 242.

edge that after avowing his love for her he had become engaged to Mrs. Custis. Stung by this taunt, George threw all restraint aside and told her unmistakably that she was the one he really loved:

Fort Cumberland, September 12, 1758

Dear Madam:

Yesterday I was honor'd with your *short* but very agreeable favour of the first Inst. How joyfully I catch at the happy occasion of renewing a corrispondance which I fear'd was disrelish'd on your part, I leave to time that never failing Expositor of all things, and to a Monitor equally as faithful in my own Breast to Testifie. In silence I now express my Joy. Silence, which in some cases—I wish the present—speaks more intelligably than the sweetest Eloquence.

If you allow that any honour can be deriv'd from my opposition to our present System of management, you destroy the merit of it entirely in me by attributing my anxiety to the animating prospect of possessing Mrs. Custis, when, I need not name it, guess yourself, should not my own Honour and Country's welfare be the ex[in]citement? 'Tis true I profess myself a votary to Love. I acknowledge that a Lady is in the case; and, further, I confess that this Lady is known to you. Yes, Madam, as well as she is to one who is too sensible of her Charms to deny the Power whose influence he feels and must ever submit to. I feel the force of her amiable beauties in the recollection of a thousand tender passages that I could wish to obliterate till I am bid to revive them; but Experience alas! sadly reminds me how impossible this is, and evinces an Opinion, which I have long entertained, that there is a Destiny which has the sovereign controul of our actions, not to be resisted by the strongest efforts of Human Nature.

You have drawn me, my dear Madam, or rather I have drawn myself, into an honest confession of a Simple Fact. Misconstrue not my meaning, 'tis obvious; doubt it not, nor expose it. The world has no business to know the object of my Love, declared in this manner to you, when I want to conceal it. One thing above all things in this world I wish to know, and only one person of your acquaintance can solve me that, or guess my meaning. But adieu to this till happier times, if I ever shall see them. The hours at present are melancholy dull. Neither the rugged toils of war, no[r] the gentler conflict of A[ssembly] B[alls], is in my choice. I dare believe you are as happy as you say, I wish I was happy also. Mirth, good humor, ease of mind, and—what else?—cannot fail to render you so and consummate your wishes. . . .

I cannot easily forgive the unseasonable haste of my last express, if he deprived me thereby of a single word you intended to add. The time of the present messenger is, as the last might have been, entirely at your disposal. I can't expect to hear from my friends more than this once before the fate of the expedition will some how or other be determined. I therefore beg to know when you set out for Hampton, and when you expect to return to Belvoir again. And I should be glad also to hear of your speedy departure, as I shall thereby hope for your return before I get down. The disappointment of not seeing your family would give me much concern.[33]

This is the most ardent love letter Washington ever wrote. It is a passionate avowal of his love for Sally Fairfax. When we read of "a thousand tender passages" that had passed between him and Sally, it is apparent that

[33] *Ibid.*, II, 287-289. This letter, one of those found in the personal papers of Sally Fairfax at Bath, England, after her death, was first printed in the New York *Herald*, March 30, 1877.

their relations were no mere surface affair. They must have exchanged vows of love upon many occasions, and one cannot help reiterating the words of Rupert Hughes: "So Sally and George were on terms of intimacy. And what intimacy meant in some of those country houses on festive occasions can hardly be imagined now." [34]

An explanation of this extraordinary letter is given by a historian of the Cary family:

> Why should he [Washington] select this juncture, of all others, to make such an avowal? He was about to consummate his engagement with Mrs. Custis, the match unexceptionable in every point of view; the wedding day was scarce four months off. And if this contemplated marriage was with him more of a matter of cool judgment and esteem than of passion, did not every consideration all the more conspire to induce a man of more than ordinary prudence and honor to veil carefully the real state of his feelings? What was the object of this declaration at such a time, to a married woman?
>
> Ah, the secret spring of an action so extraordinary cannot be doubted. It is a sudden revolt in the soul of a man intensely wrought who has nerved himself to take a step against which his rebellious heart makes its final emphatic protest, and who, before he crosses the irrevocable Rubicon of matrimony, pauses to falter forth his real, feeling soul in a piteous sort of frenzy to the long unattainable love of his life, to clasp his hopeless attachment in the mad embrace, as it were, ere he parts with his cherished ideal forever.[35]

This communication of September 12 was not the last letter that George sent to Sally from camp. On September

25 he wrote her a short note in response to one of her obscurely worded letters. She was an expert in using phrases that had two meanings, and it was difficult for George to cope with this artistry in verbal fencing. If she would only write in homespun language that would convey a message of simple affection, he would answer her in a rush of ardent words that might storm the door of her heart; but she was fearful of this very action and continued to write like the Delphic oracle. Plainly puzzled by her tantalizing tactics, he sent her a final letter in which he despairingly confessed his failure to understand the tenor of her correspondence:

25th September, 1758

Dear Madam:

Do we still misunderstand the true meaning of each other's Letters? I think it must appear so, tho' I would feign hope the contrary as I cannot speak plainer without —But I'll say no more and leave you to guess the rest. . . .

I should think my time more agreeable spent, believe me, in playing a part in Cato, with the company you mention, and myself doubly happy in being the Juba to such a Marcia, as you must make. . . .[36]

[36] Sally's note apparently referred to friends who were visiting at Belvoir and their readings of Addison's play *Cato*. In the play Juba describes the charms of Marcia thus:

> The virtuous Marcia towers above her sex.
> True, she is fair (Oh how divinely fair!)
> But still the lovely maid improves her charms
> With inward greatness, unaffected wisdom
> And sanctity of manners. . . .
> Oh, Marcia, let me hope thy kind concerns
> And gentle wishes follow me to battle!
> The thought will give new vigor to my arm.

One thing more and then have done. You ask if I am not tired at the length of your Letter? No Madam, I am not, nor never can be while the Lines are an Inch asunder to bring you in haste to the end of the Paper. You may be tird of mine by this. Adieu, dear Madam, you possibly will hear something of me, or from me before we shall meet. I must beg the favour of you to make my Compliments to Colo. Cary and the Ladies with you. . . .[37]

It is apparent that thoughts of his approaching marriage to Mrs. Custis could not keep George's impetuous pen from writing love letters to Sally Fairfax. It would have taken merely the lightest word of encouragement from Sally to change the picture completely, and the whole history of America would have been different. But for Washington this would have taken a long glance into the future, and it is hardly likely that in September, 1758, he gave much thought about the years in distant prospect. His thoughts were concentrated on Sally and the present. Sally was fully familiar with this fact, but his warmth could not melt her resolve to keep on playing at love with no specific goal in sight. George had played this waiting game for a decade, however, and he wanted something more than a lady's notes, no matter how delicately scented or filled with romantic allusions.

Washington decided to resign his commission as colonel of the Virginia Regiment and retire to Mount Vernon where he could forget his former dreams of military renown.[38] The resignation, his seventh in four years, was duly submitted, and he received the "Humble Address of the Officers of the Virginia Regiment," [39] a tribute

[37] Washington, *Writings,* ed. Fitzpatrick, II, 292-294.
[38] See *ibid.,* II, 316-317.
[39] *Ibid.,* II, 316.

that touched him deeply. It is a significant fact that during his military career George was able to win and hold the affection of the officers who served under him.

When he returned to Mount Vernon he called at Belvoir and saw Sally Fairfax, who had returned from Hampton. Although she must have seen desire staring hungrily out of his eyes, she made no overture for a new relationship, and he knew that their love idyl had reached its end.

On January 6, 1759, he married Martha Custis. The wedding took place at the White House, the fine home Mrs. Custis owned on the York River. The clergyman who officiated was the Reverend David Mossom. According to Bishop Meade, the clergyman himself was a shy person who kept his eyes glued to his prayerbook and would not look at Mrs. Custis, who was a very colorful sight. Says one description:

> Nothing ever could have been more elegant than Washintgon's bride, who cast aside all traditions about the severity of a widow's wedding garb and decked herself in brave and becoming finery: cascades of rich "point" garnished her gown, and pearls glistened in her ears and around her throat and wrists.[40]

George was also dressed in the height of fashion. He was in a civilian costume of blue cloth lined with red silk and trimmed with silver. Beneath was an embroidered white satin waistcoat. His knee breeches were fastened with buckles of gold, as were his shoes. He wore at his side a straight dress sword. His hair was powdered, and on his hands were white gloves that are preserved in the Masonic Museum at Alexandria, Virginia.

[40] Robins, *op. cit.*, p. 39.

On marrying Martha, George immediately assumed control over her property. By law he acquired administration over one-third of her former husband's property, and he was careful to go to court and secure letters of administration with reference to the remaining two-thirds. He assumed full responsibility for Mrs. Custis' children by her previous marriage, and time would prove him a most dutiful and loving stepfather.

After the wedding the couple spent three months at the Six Chimney House, Martha's house in Williamsburg, and then went to Mount Vernon. This was the occasion of further festivities. In these Washington was never backward. According to the diary of John London of Wilmington, George could handle his liquor exceedingly well:

> Gen'l Hamilton told us that Gen'l Washington, notwithstanding his perfect regularity and love of decorum, could bear to drink more wine than most people. He loved to make a procrastinated dinner—made it a rule to drink a glass of wine with every one at the table and yet always drank 3-4 or more glasses of wine after dinner, according to his company—and every night took a pint of cream and toasted crust for supper.[41]

It must have been a somewhat embarrassing moment when George William Fairfax and the exquisite Sally first paid a visit to Mount Vernon. But Sally handled the situation with her usual finesse, and Washington's diaries mention many visits between Belvoir and Mount Vernon. One cannot help wondering whether during these visits Washington ever seized an opportunity to whisper a word

[41] Quoted in Charles M. Andrews, *Colonial Folkways* (New York, 1921), pp. 108, 116.

of affection to Sally, and whether she ever playfully pinched his arm or walked so close beside him that she could feel the tremor of his body when an old love tugged at the strings of his heart.

But his life at Mount Vernon seemed tranquil and happy. He called Martha "my dearest Patsy," while she called him her "old man." According to one biographer, George always wore around his neck a little chain with a miniature of Martha hanging on it.[42] When he was called to the wars, he sent for her to be with him during every interlude in the fighting, and he retired to solitude with her at every opportunity. In commenting upon Washington's married life, Meade Minnegerode remarks: "That for long years George and Martha shared each other's lives, in complete serenity and sympathy, and with ever increasing affection and devotion, remains perhaps his greatest and most admirable achievement, and her most noteworthy accomplishment. For he never forgot Sally Fairfax."[43]

This comment is entirely true. On a July morning in 1798, Sally stood at her writing cabinet in her home in Lansdowne Crescent, Bath, England, and slowly read a letter from Mount Vernon. It was from George Washington, who was nearing the end of his days. But he had never forgotten the bright years of his youth, and the golden chain of that memorable decade he had no desire to break. As Sally Fairfax read the first paragraph of this letter from Mount Vernon, she knew that George Washington still loved her.

[42] Hughes, *op. cit.*, I, 477.
[43] Meade Minnegerode, *Some American Ladies, Seven Informal Biographies* (New York, 1926), p. 9.

Mount Vernon, 16 May, 1798

My dear Madam:

Five and twenty years have nearly passed away since I have considered myself as the permanent resident at this place, or have been in a situation to indulge myself in a familiar intercourse with my friends by letter or otherwise. During this period so many important events have occurred and such changes in men and things have taken place as the compass of a letter would give you but an inadequate idea of. *None of which events, however, nor all of them together, have been able to eradicate from my mind the recollection of those happy moments, the happiest in my life, which I have enjoyed in your company.*[44]

The descriptive phrase "the happiest in my life" tells more clearly than any other words the real love story in the life of George Washington. There is no doubt that his marriage to Martha Custis brought him years of quiet contentment at Mount Vernon, but one cannot help wondering what would have been the result had Washington cast caution aside and taken Sally to his estate at Mount Vernon, daring his critics to do their worst. It would have been the greatest love story in American history. With Sally at his side, George might not have taken long years to defeat the British armies during the American Revolution. At times, inspiration can work wonders. If Lord Nelson had repulsed the warm advances of Lady Hamilton, there might never have been the glorious victory at Trafalgar.

[44] Quoted in Cary, *op. cit.*, pp. 54-55. Italics are Washington's.

two

Benjamin Franklin
[1706-1790]

THE MANY-SIDED FRANKLIN

It is difficult to distill the essence of Franklin's personality in the space of a few paragraphs. He was many things to many people. Estimates of the man vary from extravagant adulation to rancorous criticism, though his friends were more numerous and more articulate than his enemies. In his family circle he aroused deep devotion. To his sister, Jane Mecom, he was almost a deity: "I think it is not profanity to compare you to our Blessed Saviour who employed much of his time while here on earth in doing good to the body as well as souls of men." Elizabeth Hubbard, the stepdaughter of his brother John, warned him that if he continued to live his good life he would find himself "alone in Heaven." Sir Samuel Romilly expressed the opinion that Franklin was "one of the best and most eminent men of the present age," while Lord Kames remarked that he was a "man who makes a great figure in the learned world; and who would make a still greater figure for benevolence and candor, were virtue as much regarded in this declining age as knowledge." And finally, George Washington, who spoke from intimate acquaintance, paid him the following tribute: "If to be venerated for benevolence, if to be admired for talents, if to be esteemed for patriotism, if to be loved for philanthropy, can gratify the human mind, you must have the pleasing consolation to know, that you have not lived in vain." [1]

But Franklin was not free from sharp criticism. To Arthur Lee he was "the meanest of all mean men, the most corrupt of all corrupt men," while Stephen Sayre regarded him as a "great villain." To John Adams he was the "vainest man and the falsest character I have ever met in life." [2] The French critic Sainte-Beuve thought Franklin lacked idealism: "All ideal is lacking in this healthy, upright, able, frugal, laborious nature of Franklin. There is in him no fine flower of enthusiams, tenderness, sacrifice. . . . He brings every thing down to arithmetic and strict reality, assigning no part to human imagination." D. H. Lawrence was even more critical. He dismissed Franklin as a "snuff-colored little man" who set up an "unlovely, snuff-colored ideal." This pattern-American, "this dry,

---

[1] Quoted in William C. Bruce, *Benjamin Franklin Self-Revealed* (New York, 1942, 2 vols.), I, 2-23.

[2] Quoted in Page Smith, *John Adams* (Garden City, 1962, 2 vols.), II, 622.

moral, utilitarian little democrat has done more to ruin old Europe than any Russian nihilist." [3]

Sainte-Beuve and later Lawrence must have known Franklin mainly through the pages of the *Autobiography* and *Poor Richard's Almanack* with their emphasis on scrimping and saving. It is easy to confuse the real Franklin with poor Richard of the *Almanack* and to believe that he generally viewed life through the clouded lens of materialism. Other more righteous critics were shocked by some of Franklin's Rabelaisian *jeux d'esprit:* "Polly Baker's Speech," the letter on "The Choice of a Mistress," and the "Essay on Perfumes," for example. "The Choice of a Mistress" was long regarded as particularly wicked, and after the Franklin collection of manuscripts was purchased by the federal government and turned over to the Department of State for safekeeping, this letter was seldom shown to historians. [4]

The note struck in these particular essays had been sounded before in some of the writings of Dean Swift, but it was a note more appreciated in sophisticated London than in prim Philadelphia. Moreover, the fact that Franklin had an illegitimate son, William Franklin, for whose unorthodox birth he never apologized caused many eyebrows to be raised, and when this wayward son caused history to repeat itself and presented Franklin with an illegitimate grandson, many good people thought they had seen everything.

It is true that Franklin sometimes wrote his own code of

[3] Quoted in Lewis Leary, Introduction to Benjamin Franklin, *Autobiography* (New York, 1962), p. ix.

[4] See Benjamin Franklin, *Papers,* ed. Leonard W. Labaree and Whitfield J. Bell, Jr. (New Haven, 1959-1962, 5 vols.), III, 29.

morals and bothered little about the opinions of his fellow citizens concerning his conduct; but in most cases he did not advertise his actions, keeping a discreet silence about his infractions of prevailing conventions. He never took the trouble formally to marry Deborah Rogers, whose absent husband, like some troublesome jack-in-the-box, might pop up at the most embarrassing moment and prefer charges of bigamy against Deborah. In this regard Franklin was content to live dangerously, and Deborah, who had little formal education and less culture, seemed to satisfy him with her strong emphasis upon sensual pleasures.

EARLY LIFE

As one studies the complex personality of Franklin, it is apparent that despite his Boston birth (on January 6, 1706) the Puritan way of life had little attraction for him. He had few inhibitions to check his warm impulses, and seldom did the fearsome shadow of sin put fear into his heart. He was a normal, lighthearted lad, and the windows of his soul looked out upon the sunny slopes of life, not the dark valleys that tortured the minds of stern New Englanders like Jonathan Edwards or Samuel Sewall. He had little interest in religious sects and in doctrinal theology. "Honest heretics" like Doctor Priestley were close to his heart: "I think all the heretics I have known have been virtuous men. They have the virtue of fortitude, or they would not venture to own their heresy, . . . and they have not, like orthodox sinners, such a number of friends to excuse or justify them." [5]

[5] Quoted in Bruce, *op. cit.,* I, 67.

Franklin's family was not among the mighty in the New England community, and he had no lofty family pretensions to sustain. His father was a tallow chandler of very modest means who had to practice the strictest economy in maintaining his large family. Franklin remembered when there were thirteen members around the family table and the keen air of New England winters had a way of sharpening appetites.

Franklin's father nursed high hopes for his youngest son, who at eight years of age was placed in a grammar school to prepare him eventually for the ministry. But economic pressure upset these plans, and after one year Benjamin was transferred to a private school that emphasized writing and arithmetic. Ben did his reading at home. When he failed in arithmetic, his father decided that he had learned enough to help in the work of molding candles, and put him to cutting wicks and filling molds.

Ben disliked this type of work and yearned for a life of adventure. Living in Boston where ships kept returning from distant ports of all the seven seas, it was natural that the lure of faraway places should kindle his imagination. But his father was opposed to his following a career on the sea, and at the age of twelve he was apprenticed to his brother James to learn the printing trade. James had recently returned from London with a printing press and a good supply of type, and he was ready to set up in business.

Ben's printing work seemed to set his mind in the direction of composing, and he soon began to write ballads which his brother printed and he hawked about the streets of Boston. One dealt with a "Lighthouse Tragedy" and told the sad story of the demise of George Worthylake, a

keeper of the light on Beacon Island.[6] The following verse
will give an idea of its touching accents:

> Oh! George, this wild November
> We must not pass with you
> For Ruth, our fragile daughter
> Its chilly gales will rue.

For a twelve-year-old this was quite a performance, and
Ben was encouraged to write similar ballads that seemed
to please the public taste. The most popular was entitled,
"A Sailor Song on the Taking of Teach or Blackbeard
the Pirate." According to Ben these ballads "sold wonder-
fully," and this gave him an incurable desire to keep on
writing.

Inasmuch as his brother James also published a newspaper, Ben thought he might be able to have some of his
writings inserted in it. James had several friends who
helped him with this newspaper enterprise; they would
often gather in the print shop in Queen Street to discuss
their plans. Ben's sharp ears took in all these discussions.
It seemed to him quite possible that he might be able to
have one of his writings published in the *Courant* if he
put it in the form of a letter on current affairs. He decided to sign his letter with the pen name of Silence
Dogood.

His exercises in ballad writing had given him a definite verbal facility. He had no trouble writing the letter,
which he slipped under the door of the print shop. The
next morning he had the "exquisite pleasure" of hearing
the enthusiastic approval his brother's friends expressed
after they had read it. They thought it should be printed

[6] Franklin, *Papers,* I, 6.

immediately in the *Courant*. Ben wrote thirteen more Silence Dogood letters until his "small fund of Sense for such Performances was pretty well exhausted." [7]

The first of the Silence Dogood letters was published in the *Courant* on April 2, 1722, and told the story of an estimable young lady who had been left an orphan at a tender age but who had been able to arrive at her "years of discretion" without any untoward occurrence. She had been living a "chearful Country Life" and had spent her "leisure Time either in some innocent Diversion or in some shady Retirement, with the best of Company, *Books*." Her later innocent adventures were related in subsequent numbers of the *Courant*.[8]

While the Silence Dogood letters in the *Courant* attracted favorable notice, such was not the case with other "writings" that gave "offense to the Assembly"; so James Franklin was called before that body, publicly censured, and imprisoned for a month. To meet this emergency he issued an announcement that henceforth the *Courant* would be published by his brother Benjamin Franklin. But James continued to publish writings that were resented by the members of the ministry and some of the magistrates, and an order for his arrest was issued. On February 12, 1723, he gave his bond to keep the peace, and the grand jury failed to return an indictment against him. The *Courant* continued to be published over the name of Benjamin Franklin until it expired in 1726, but the nominal publisher had fled from Boston in September, 1723, and taken up his residence in Philadelphia.

[7] Franklin, *Autobiography,* p. 29.
[8] *Ibid.,* pp. 34-35.

THE CITY OF NOT-SO-BROTHERLY LOVE

A love of freedom and a strong belief that he would do better on his own in a strange city led Ben to migrate to Philadelphia that September. After some interesting adventures en route to the city of brotherly love, he finally reached his destination without any money and with no idea where he might find employment. His account of his entrance into the city is a classic which should be quoted from his *Autobiography*. He had gone into a bakeshop and asked for three pennies' worth of bread:

> He gave me, accordingly, three great puffy rolls. I was surprised at the quantity, but took it, and, having no room in my pockets, walk'd off with a roll under each arm, and eating the other. Thus I went up Market-street as far as Fourth-street, passing by the door of Mr. Read, my future wife's father; when she, standing at the door, saw me, and thought I made, as I certainly did, a most awkward, ridiculous appearance.[9]

Through the good offices of Andrew Bradford, Ben was finally able to secure a position in the print shop of Samuel Keimer. Keimer had no quarters for him, but through Keimer's intercession Ben was given a suitable lodging with Mr. Read, with the added attraction of the landlord's buxom daughter as maid of all work.

The daughter, Deborah, agreed with Alexander Pope that a little learning is a dangerous thing, and followed the safe path of general ignorance. She had a good figure,

[9] *Ibid.*, pp. 34-35.

however, and in Ben's visual arithmetic this added up to a nice sum. But his response to her physical charms had to be restrained. His financial prospects were not bright, and Ben knew full well that two cannot live as cheaply as one.

In *Poor Richard's Almanack*, Ben subsequently showed a remarkable knowledge of proverbs and wise sayings, and he deeply impressed the public with a yearly recitation of rules of conduct that were eminently sound. But in his first months in Philadelphia he did not display this wide learning, and was particularly ignorant of the ancient admonition that all that glistens is not gold; if he had used this proverb as a compass to guide him through the rough waters of Philadelphia society, he would have been spared many pains. In other words, he was inviting bait for city slickers.

One day while he was busily at work in Keimer's print shop, two gentlemen handsomely garbed in the latest fashion called to see him. One was Sir William Keith, governor of the Province of Pennsylvania, with a companion he introduced as Colonel French. The Governor was all smiles and promises. He chided Ben for not having made his presence in the province more widely known; a young man with his unusual talents should have immediate success as a printer. He invited Ben to go with him to a neighboring tavern for a cheering glass of excellent Madeira. Ben promptly accepted this impressive invitation, and when the wine had warmed their blood the Governor proposed setting Ben up in the printing business.

When Ben's prudent father would not supply part of the funds needed for the venture, Governor Keith proposed that Ben go to London and purchase equipment for the printing shop, promising that he would advance the money to cover the purchases. Ben took his promises at face value and began to plan his trip. In the weeks before he completed his preparations, he began seriously to court Deborah, who now was looking boldly at Ben over the high ramparts of her ample bosom. But Deborah's mother was one of the cautious kind, and she decided it would be wiser to postpone any steps leading toward a closer relationship between them.

PROMISES ARE EASIER MADE THAN KEPT

Ben expected to hear from Governor Keith about the promised financial help before booking passage for London. But no word came from the Governor, and Ben sailed without the money he would need to have when he reached there. He arrived in the British capital on December 24, 1724, and soon realized that the Governor's promise was an empty one which was never to be fulfilled. He now found himself in an unfamiliar city with no money. Fortunately he was able to find employment at Palmer's, a famous printing shop in Bartholomew Close, and this income made it possible for him to eke out an existence. But he had to share his small wages with a friend, James Ralph, who had accompanied him on the trip.

Ralph was an unsteady person with literary pretensions which he hoped would blossom into something worthwhile in the favorable literary climate of London. He had abandoned a wife and child in Philadelphia, and in London soon began to share his bed with an attractive milliner who preferred making love to making hats. When Ralph got a teaching position in the country at too small a salary to support the milliner, Ben kindly suggested to her that he would like to warm the spot in the bed that Ralph had occupied. The comely milliner rejected his torrid advances but readily accepted money from him for living expenses.

As a married man, Ralph was familiar with the alphabet of love-making, and his tender phrases had acted like a magnet to draw the milliner to his side. Unfortunately for Ben, his writing experience had been largely in the field of polemics, and he found that barbed phrases were not the proper ritual for seduction. When the milliner informed Ralph of Ben's amorous proposals, he became properly indignant at the attempted betrayal and served notice on Ben that he would make no effort to repay the large sum he had borrowed from him.

Chastened by this disturbing and costly experience, Ben hurriedly found new lodgings in Duke Street, opposite the Romish chapel. The odor of sanctity helped orient his mind toward things spiritual, and his new landlady was most respectable. Certainly she presented no temptation:

> She was lame in her knees with the gout, and therefore seldom stirred out of her room, so sometimes wanted company; and hers was so highly amusing to me, that I was sure to spend an evening with her whenever she desired it. Our supper was only half an anchovy each, on a very little strip of bread and butter, and half a pint of ale between us.

Another occupant of his new quarters was even more spiritual. She had given up most of her estate, reserving only £12 a year to live on. A priest visited her to confess her every day. When Ben inquired "how she, as she liv'd, could possibly find so much employment for a confessor," she blandly replied that it was impossible "to avoid vain thoughts." [10]

The company of these aged and virtuous ladies was an excellent spiritual corrective for Ben after his unfortunate experience with the milliner, and his thoughts began to turn more and more to Philadelphia, where the feminine atmosphere was not so rarefied. He had been able to save enough for passage home, and after a stormy crossing he landed in Philadelphia on October 11, 1726.

A DUBIOUS MARRIAGE AND PRIOR OFFSPRING

When Ben once more took up his abode in Philadelphia the chill of London was still in his blood, so he looked up his former feminine friend, Deborah Read, whose figure was now more span than spic and whose eyes were not the bright invitation to happiness they had been many months before. She had meanwhile married a potter named Rogers, who had become involved in debts which he had no inclination to pay. Fearing legal action, he quietly left town one night without the formality of a farewell to Deborah. With her husband nowhere in sight, she now became an attraction to men. One of these men was Ben.

But before he could seriously entertain any idea of an intimate association with Deborah, Ben would have to find profitable employment. He spent a brief period at work, again in the print shop of Samuel Keimer, and then he and Hugh Meredith set up a print shop of their own. Meredith's intemperance soon led to a dissolution of

[10] *Ibid.*, pp. 53-54.

the partnership, and Ben carried on alone. After completing a commission to print some paper currency for the state treasury, he decided to publish a newspaper. On October 2, 1729, the first number of the *Pennsylvania Gazette* made its appearance. It carried many local items, some foreign news of wide interest, and some provocative letters and essays.

When the *Gazette* seemed to be on a firm foundation, Ben once more began to think of marriage. Some arrangement with Deborah Rogers would be convenient, and at the same time she might become a real helpmate in the book and stationery store he had added to his print shop. It would be a very practical arrangement with few overtones of sentimental romance. But we will let Ben tell his own story. He had just closed the door on a brief courtship of a Miss Godfrey and was looking around for another girl to court:

I look'd round me and made overtures of acquaintance in other places; but soon found that, the business of a printer being generally thought a poor one, I was not to expect money with a wife, unless with such a one as I should not otherwise think agreeable. In the meantime, that hard-to-be-governed passion of youth hurried me frequently into intrigues with low women who fell in my way, which were attended with some expense and great inconvenience, besides a continual risque to my health by a distemper which of all things I dreaded, though by great good luck I escaped it.

A friendly correspondence as neighbors and old acquaintances had continued between me and Mrs. Read's family, who all had a regard for me from the time of my first lodging in their house. I was often invited there and consulted in their affairs, wherein I sometimes was of service. I piti'd poor Miss Read's unfortunate situation, who was generally dejected . . . and avoided company. I considered my giddiness and inconstancy when in London as in a great degree the cause of her unhappiness. . . . Our mutual affection was revived, but there were now great objections to our union. The match [with Rogers] indeed was looked upon as invalid, a preceding wife being said to be living in England; but this could not be easily prov'd, because of the distance; and tho' there was a report of his death, it was not certain. . . . We ventured, however, over all these difficulties, and I took her to wife, September 1, 1730. None of the inconveniences happened that we had apprehended; she proved a good and faithful helpmate, assisted me much by attending the shop.[11]

It is obvious that there was no formal marriage ceremony; at least, there is no record of any such ceremony in Christ Church, of which Deborah was a member. The law against bigamy was one not to be lightly defined. The union between Ben and Deborah was probably a common-law marriage, to which Ben had no objection. Indeed he did not think much about the marriage ceremony as a prelude to intercourse, as his two illegitimate children clearly proved. Shortly after he took Deborah "to wife," he surprised her one day by bringing into the household an illegitimate son whom he called William. Deborah had little affection for this new addition to the family circle. According to Daniel Fisher, who lived with the Franklins, one day when William passed the house Deborah scowled at him darkly and whispered to Fisher: "There goes the greatest Villain upon Earth." [12]

11 *Ibid.*, pp. 70-71.
12 Quoted in *Pennsylvania Magazine of History*, XVII, 276.

But Franklin always regarded his son William with affection, and he took him to London during his first mission to England and entered him for study in the Inns of Court. Moreover, he did not protest when in 1760 William suddenly presented him with an illegitimate grandson, William Temple Franklin, usually called Temple. The upbringing of this grandson was taken over exclusively by Ben and the boy hardly knew his father, who later became famous when appointed by the Crown as governor of New Jersey. Temple made his home with his grandfather during Franklin's second mission to England, and he accompanied him to Paris during his momentous mission to France.

If Deborah's patience was sorely tried when Franklin brought William home, it is easy to imagine her dismay when he introduced her to his illegitimate daughter. Little is known of this female offspring, and biographers of Franklin have usually avoided any mention of her, but the fact of her existence was made known in a series of letters published in the appendix of Sydney George Fisher's *The True Benjamin Franklin*. Ben obviously warmed more beds in Philadelphia than most people realized.

Ben's illegitimate son was a constant joy to him during his early years, and later a valued companion. The same is true of his illegitimate grandson. Of his illegitimate great-grandson not much is known beyond the fact that there was one.

Deborah gave Franklin two children, one a boy who died when he was still a small child and the other a daughter, Sally, to whom he was deeply devoted. But the family atmosphere at times must have been depressing, and it is not strange that Ben apparently enjoyed his two missions to England, which removed him from Philadel-

phia and from Deborah for fifteen years.[13] In London he
had delightful quarters at 7 Craven Street with the charming and solicitous Mrs. Margaret Stevenson. His daily
companions were men and women who were his intellectual equals, and the years slipped by with pleasant
speed. Deborah tried to keep in touch with him by frequent letters which must have reminded him that the real
gulf between them was as wide as the broad Atlantic.
Her penmanship left much to be desired, while the style
and spelling must have made Ben at times wonder if she
were writing in English or in the dialect of some Indian
tribe that still lingered in the environs of Philadelphia.
The following letter is a good example of the distorted
missives that Ben received from Deborah:

October ye 29, 1773

My dear child

I have bin very much distrest a boute as I did not oney
letter nor one word from you nor did I hear one word from
oney bodey that you wrote to So I must submit and in-
dever to submit to what I ame to hair I did write by Capt
Folkner to you but he is gone doun and when I read it
over I did not like it and so if this dont send it I shante like
it as I donte send you oney news nor I donte go abrode.

I shall tell you what consernves myself our yonegest
Grandson is the finest child as alive he has had the small

---

[13] The following description of Deborah from Bernard Fay, *Franklin, the Apostle of Modern Times* (New York, 1929), p. 233, indicates her
rather pitiful attempt to live up to her advanced social station: "On Sun-
day she put on fine clothes and when she left for church, wearing her
double necklace of golden beads, accompanied by her pretty little
blonde-haired girl, and followed by two Negro slaves, she cut a good
figure, and the neighbors had to admit that she looked like the wife of
somebody."

Pox and had it very fine and got abrod agen Capt All will tell you a boute him Benj Franklin Beache but as it is so deficall to writ I have desered him to tell you I have sente a squerel for your friend and wish her better luck.[14]

It is obvious that Deborah would hardly have fitted into the London circles that Ben frequented, and perhaps it was fortunate that he had his illegitimate son and grandson as greatly treasured companions during his long absences abroad.

THE *Pennsylvania Gazette, Poor Richard's Almanack,* AND OTHER WRITINGS

The *Pennsylvania Gazette,* which Ben began to publish in October, 1729, quickly became a journalistic success, and he gave much thought to ways of improving its appeal to readers. Soon the *Gazette* was filled with colorful stories of people about town:

Friday Night last, a certain St-n-c-tt-r was, it seems, in a fair way of dying the Death of a Nobleman; for being caught Napping with another Man's Wife, the injur'd Husband took the Advantage of his being fast asleep, and with a Knife began very diligently to cut off his Head. But the instrument not being equal to the intended Operation, much struggling prevented Success; and he was oblig'd to content himself for the present with bestowing on the Aggressor a sound Drubbing. The Gap made in the Side of the St-n-c-tt-r's Neck, tho' deep, is not thought dangerous, but some People admire, that when the Person offended

[14] Quoted in Sydney G. Fisher, *The True Benjamin Franklin* (Philadelphia, 1899), p. 117.

had so fair and suitable an Opportunity, it did not enter into his Head to turn St-n-c-tt-r himself.

A week later the *Gazette* was able to come up with another equally interesting item:

> We hear, that on Tuesday last, a certain C-n-table having made an Agreement with a Neighbouring Female, to *Watch* with her that Night; she promised to leave a Window open for him to come in at; but he going his Rounds in the dark, unluckily mistook the Window, and got into a Room where another Woman was in bed, and her Husband it seems lying on a Couch not far distant. The good Woman perceiving presently by the extraordinary Fondness of her Bedfellow that it could not possibly be her Husband, made so much Disturbance as to wake the good man; who finding somebody had got into his Place without his Leave, began to lay about him unmercifully; and 'twas thought, that had not our poor mistaken Galant, call'd out manfully for Help (as if he were commanding Assistance in the King's name) and thereby raised the Family, he would have stood no more Chance for his Life between the Wife and Husband, than a captive L---- between the two Thumb Nails.[15]

These fables in the *Gazette* boosted the circulation considerably, but Ben had other ideas for making money through his print shop. Other printers were making handsome incomes through the publication of almanacs. Some of them had an annual sale of 10,000 copies, and Ben realized that it would not be difficult for him to publish one. On December 19, 1732, he advertised the publication of

[15] Franklin, *Papers*, I, 217.

Poor Richard's Almanack.[16] In some ways it was quite original. It was not only filled with the usual dubious prophecies about the weather, but it also had some Swiftian hoaxes in which he predicted to the very hour and minute the deaths of his rival almanac publishers and others. He awoke the interest of a wide circle of readers by printing a large number of verses, proverbs, and aphorisms which were more pointed and more humorous than those printed in other almanacs. In this new venture he was singularly successful, and *Poor Richard's Almanack* sold more than the hoped-for 10,000 copies annually. Ben had at last found a sure road to riches.[17]

After writing for some years for the *Gazette* fables that squinted obliquely at lust, Ben decided in 1745 to extend these fables into letters or speeches and retain the salacious flavor. He was one of the first American writers to emphasize sex.

In June, 1745, Ben wrote a fictitious letter that for many decades distinctly embarrassed his many admirers. In 1882 the United States Government purchased the Franklin collection of manuscripts from the collector Henry Stevens. The librarian of the Department of State was startled to discover a second version of Franklin's letter relative to "the Choice of a Mistress." For a considerable time this interesting document was shown to eager historians with obvious reluctance. As Paul L. Ford explained to a friend, the Franklin letter "was kept very

[16] See Paul L. Ford, ed., *The Sayings of Poor Richard* (New York, 1890); S. A. Gallacher, "Franklin's Way to Wealth," *Journal of English and Germanic Philology,* XLVIII, 220-251.

[17] Many copies of the make-up of this almanac are reproduced in Franklin, *Papers,* I and II.

private," and when Bigelow wished to include it in his edition of Franklin's *Works,* permission was refused by Secretary of State Thomas F. Bayard. He did, however, give a copy to an important New York politician and friend, who read it aloud at a famous dinner party in New York.

Because of this secrecy the letter became an object of increasing curiosity, but no nineteenth-century editor or biographer offended the public taste by printing it. John B. McMaster, the distinguished historian at the University of Pennsylvania, expressed the opinion that the letter was "unhappily too indecent to print." [18] Paul L. Ford feared that it would "shock modern taste." [19] Albert H. Smyth, in volume I of his edition of the *Writings of Benjamin Franklin,* discussed the Franklin manuscripts and remarked that there were certain ones whose publication would "not be tolerated by the public sentiment of the present age." [20] In 1926 Phillips Russell printed the whole letter in his biography of Franklin,[21] and fifteen years later Max Schuster published it without any qualms in his well-known anthology, *A Treasury of the World's Great Letters.* This much-discussed and sharply criticized letter on "The Choice of a Mistress" reads as follows:

My dear Friend,

I know of no Medicine fit to diminish the violent natural inclinations you mention; and if I did, I think I should not

[18] John B. McMaster, *Benjamin Franklin as a Man of Letters* (Boston, 1887), p. 266.

[19] Paul L. Ford, *The Many-Sided Franklin* (New York, 1899), p. 410.

[20] Benjamin Franklin, *Writings,* ed. Albert H. Smyth (New York, 1905-1907, 10 vols.), I, 171.

[21] Phillips Russell, *Benjamin Franklin, the First Civilized American* (New York, 1926), pp. 171-173.

communicate it to you. Marriage is the proper Remedy. It
is the most natural State of Man, and therefore the State in
which you are most likely to find solid Happiness. . . .
But if you will not take this Counsel, and persist in thinking a Commerce with the Sex inevitable, then I repeat my
former Advice, that in all your Amours you should prefer
old Women to young ones. You call this a Paradox, and demand my Reasons. They are these:

1. Because as they have more Knowledge of the World
   and their Minds are better stor'd with Observations,
   their Conversation is more improving and more last-
   ingly agreeable.

2. Because when Women cease to be handsome, they
   study to be good. To maintain their Influence over
   Men, they supply the Diminution of Beauty by an
   Augmentation of Utility. They learn to do a 1000
   Services small and great, and are the most tender and
   useful of all Friends when you are sick. Thus they
   continue amiable. And hence there is hardly such a
   thing to be found as an old Woman who is not a good
   Woman.

3. Because there is no hazard of Children, which irregu-
   larly produc'd may be attended with much Inconvenience.

4. Because thro' more Experience, they are more prudent and discreet in conducting an Intrigue to prevent
   Suspicion. The Commerce with them is therefore
   safer with regard to your Reputation. And with regard to theirs, if the Affair should happen to be
   known, considerate People might be rather inclin'd
   to excuse an old Woman who would kindly take care
   of a young Man, form his Manners by her good Counsels, and prevent his ruining his Health and Fortune
   among mercenary Prostitutes.

5. Because in every Animal that walks upright, the De-
   ficiency of the Fluids that fill the Muscles appears first

in the highest Part; The Face first grows lank and wrinkled; then the Neck, then the Breast and Arms; the lower Parts continuing to the last as plump as ever: So that Covering all above with a Basket, and regarding only what is below the Girdle, it is impossible of two Women to know an old from a young one. And as in the dark all Cats are grey, the Pleasure of corporal Enjoyment with an old Woman is at least equal, and frequently superior, every Knack being by Practice capable of Improvement.

6. Because the Sin is less. The debauching of a Virgin may be her Ruin, and make her for Life unhappy.

7. Because the Compunction is less. The having made a young Girl *miserable* may give you frequent bitter Reflections; none of which can attend the making an old Woman *happy*.

8thly and Lastly. They are *so grateful*.

Thus much for my Paradox. But still I advise you to marry directly; being sincerely,

Your affectionate Friend.[22]

It is apparent that Franklin occasionally used this fictitious letter as a conversation piece to cheer the spirits of his companions. When he went on his mission to Canada in April, 1776, the other members of the commission were Samuel Chase, a member of the Continental Congress, Charles Carroll of Carrollton, an influential Catholic layman, and John Carroll, a Jesuit priest. The purpose of the mission was to win the good will of the Canadian people to the American cause. The populace of Quebec Province was supposed to be unhappy with English rule because of the Quebec Act of 1774, and it was believed that Charles and John Carroll, who were Catholics and

[22] Franklin, *Papers*, III, 27-31.

who had been educated in France, might be able to per-
suade large numbers of the Canadian Catholics to make
some move in favor of union with the American colonies.
It was a drive to win a fourteenth colony.

The mission was a failure, and Franklin, who was seventy, had a difficult time enduring the rigors of the trip. In
order to speed these unhappy hours, Franklin demonstrated
his arts as a conversationalist. He rehearsed for the commissioners some of his writings, and even referred to his
letter on "The Choice of a Mistress." To the Jesuit priest,
John Carroll, mention of this letter probably seemed in-
appropriate, but the other commissioners did not seem to
mind. In a letter to Franklin dated August 12, 1777,
Charles Carroll, after expressing the hope that Franklin's
flow of spirits was still at flood tide, remarked: "Mr. John
Carroll and Chase are both well; the latter is now at Congress, and has been so fully and constantly employed
that I believe he has not had leisure to refute your reasons
in favor of the old ladies." [23] There was no comment from
John Carroll, who later became the first Catholic arch-
bishop in the United States.

Another *jeu d'esprit* with which Franklin may have
cheered the lagging spirits of the American commissioners to Canada was the "Speech of Polly Baker," which he
wrote in 1747. This piece of imaginative writing was
printed in England almost immediately after completion
without any mention of Franklin's authorship, and it became quite popular in America. In 1749 the English Deist
Peter Annet included Polly Baker's alleged speech in his
Social Bliss Considered, a monograph that dealt with marriage, fornication, and divorce. From this book the Abbé
Raynal took the speech and used it extensively in his *His-*

[23] Quoted in Bruce, *op. cit.,* II, 529.

toire philosophique et politique, which he published in
1770. Raynal apparently had no idea that Polly Baker was
a fictitious person or that Franklin was really the author of
the speech. But through Raynal and others it soon became known throughout Europe.

The speech was supposed to have been made "before a
Court of Judicature at Connecticut, near Boston," where
Polly Baker was being prosecuted for the fifth time for
having a bastard child. The trial ended on a note of poetic
justice. In a postscript appended to the version printed in
the *American Museum* (1787, I, 243-245), the following
statement is made: "This judicious address influenced the
court to dispense with her punishment, and induced
one of her judges to marry her the next day. She supported an irreproachable character, and had fifteen children by her husband." [24]

It is amazing that an essay about a fictitious character
could have been accepted as reality by many thousands
of persons both in America and in Europe and as a true
picture of American customs.[25] In his *Poor Richard's Almanack* Franklin had perpetrated many hoaxes, and their
success must have induced him to try them on a larger
scale.

On April 17, 1746, the *Gazette* announced the publication of a pamphlet entitled "Reflections on Courtship and
Marriage." It is important as indicating Franklin's frame
of mind when dealing with sex and love. In the popular
mind it reinforced the impression of many that Franklin
was a person of shady morals and low tastes. One paragraph from the "Reflections," stressing the importance of

[24] Franklin, *Papers,* III, 120-125.
[25] See Max Hall, *Benjamin Franklin and Polly Baker: The History
of a Literary Deception* (Chapel Hill, 1960).

careful manners and dress between husband and wife,
will reveal Franklin's indebtedness to Dean Swift's de-
scriptions of the vulgar and coarse:

> Let us survey the morning dress of some women. Down-
> stairs they come, pulling up their ungartered, dirty stock-
> ings; slipshod, with naked heels peeping out; no stays or
> other decent conveniency, but all flipflop; a sort of a clout
> thrown about the neck, without form or decency; the
> frowzy hair hanging in sweaty ringlets, staring like Medusa
> with her serpents; shrugging up her petticoats, that are
> sweeping the ground and scarce tied on; hands unwashed,
> teeth furred, and eyes crusted—but I beg your pardon,
> I'll go no farther with this sluttish picture, which I am
> afraid has already turned your stomach.[26]

It is likely that Franklin was able to draw this unlovely
feminine picture in such detail because in his own household he had seen Deborah play the role many times. She
could not be his companion in pursuits of the mind, and
as she grew older and her physical charms faded, it is
quite likely that she was not so careful in her early morning dress as she had been when Ben, in the prime of his
passion, took her "to wife."

A FEMININE FRIENDSHIP IN BOSTON

When Franklin became absorbed in public life, it was inevitable that he was frequently away from Philadelphia
on official trips. In the fall of 1754 he traveled to Boston
on post office business, and while there he met a young

---

[26] Quoted in Carl Van Doren, *Benjamin Franklin* (New York,
1938), p. 153.

lady of twenty-three, Catherine Ray, who was a vision of charm, beauty, and intelligence. Until this time Ben's correspondence had been with men in public office or important personages throughout the colonies. In 1754 he was just forty-eight—still young enough to dream dreams and harbor rosy hankerings.

Catherine Ray was in Boston on a visit to her sister Judith. She was a person of evident refinement, and her quick intelligence responded to Franklin's unusual mental gifts. A bond was soon established between them. It was the first time since his marriage that Franklin's interest had been deeply stirred, and for a while he forgot the home fires in Philadelphia and Deborah's aging charms. He and Catherine Ray left Boston on December 30, 1754, and began a leisurely trip to Westerly, Rhode Island, where Catherine's sister Anna lived. From there Franklin accompanied Catherine to a point from which she could take a boat to Block Island, her home.

Writing of this trip, Carl Van Doren remarks: "Somewhere he watched her making sugar plums and said her hands were sweet; somewhere he talked to her of favours which she refused him, though she was rather pleased than vexed by his boldness." [27] This was the first time that Ben had asked the girl for favors, and though they were denied him, he was apparently never slapped for his advances. Indeed, instead of reproving him, Catherine archly remarked that he was a "conjurer" who had left her "under a spell." As Bernard Fay observes:

> Franklin put his family behind him and lived again in his past: in the oblivion of his old dreams and new desires; he forgot Deborah and the loud, vulgar atmosphere of his

[27] *Ibid.,* p. 234.

home, to abandon himself to this unusual feeling, to this smiling and effulgent tenderness which slowly rose and expanded in him. While Katy Ray prepared sugar plums for him, telling him all the while of a handsome Spaniard who had stirred her heart, Franklin dreamed,—Franklin, who for so long a time had only thought and acted. This young girl of New England gave him that sweet melancholy, that elegant tenderness, half-libertine, half-paternal, which was so fashionable at the time. . . . He felt a strange mist over his eyes one night, when he bade farewell to Kayt. It was an evening in winter, and she left on a little boat to visit her mother, who lived on an island; Franklin stood on the bank a long time to watch the boat, and as it faded from his sight he felt deliciously disconsolate.[28]

There was no doubt that Ben left Katy "under a spell." She felt greatly flattered that an important colonial official was paying such pointed attention to her. Her denial of her favors was obviously halfhearted, for as soon as she arrived home she wrote him a letter in which she made some "indiscreet" admissions. This and subsequent tender avowals of affection were an indication that she was his for the asking, but Ben now got cold feet, and the letters are missing from his files. In a cautious letter to Catherine on March 4, 1755, he told her how he had watched her little skiff with anxious eyes until it disappeared in the night. He had left New England "slowly, and with great Reluctance. . . . I almost forgot I had a Home." After some Puritan words about the pleasures of his home, he returned to some fair words for her:

Persons subject to the *Hyp* complain of the North-East Wind as increasing their Malady. But since you promised

[28] Fay, op. cit., pp. 246-247.

to send me Kisses in that Wind, and I find you as good as
your Word, it is to me the gayest Wind that blows and
gives me the best Spirits. I write this during a N. East
Storm of Snow, the greatest we have had this Winter. Your
favours come mixed with the Snowy Fleeces, which are
as pure as your Virgin Innocence, white as your lovely
Bosom—and as cold.[29]

The day before he wrote this letter to Catherine she
wrote him a second one, and this was followed shortly by
two more; but he was involved in the myriad details consequent on Braddock's defeat and did not find time to
answer them. On June 28 she wrote a fifth letter which is
filled with her anxieties about his welfare. His silence had
caused her

. . . a vast deal of uneasiness and occasioned many tears,
for surely I have wrote too much and you are affronted
with me, or have not received my letters, in which I have
said a thousand things that nothing should have tempted
me to [have] said to anybody else, for I knew they would
be safe with you. I'll only beg the favour of one line—
what is become of my letters. Tell me you are well and
forgive and love me one-thousandth part so well as I do
you, and then I will be contented and promise an amend-
ment. It is with the greatest reluctance I shall finish my
letter without telling you of some great alterations since
my last. But you have my promise, so I will pray God to
bless you with the best of blessings and subscribe myself,
dear sir, your most sincere, affectionate, and obliged friend.
Pray take care of your health and accept the sugar plums.
They are every one sweetened as you used to like.[30]

[29] Quoted in Franklin, *Papers,* V, 502-504.
[30] Quoted in Van Doren, *op. cit.,* pp. 236-237.

Catherine's expressions of affection are unrestrained because in another letter to her in March or April Ben had informed her that she could "write freely everything you think fit, without the least Apprehension of any Person's seeing your Letters but myself." But he was now an important public official, so in his letters to her he would have to be discreet. "I shall say less than I think, and end this Letter cooly in the plain common form, with only Dear Miss, Your humble servant, B. Franklin." [31]

Catherine Ray had taken Ben at his word, and the ardent affection smiling at him through every line of her letter of June 28 disturbed him. He could see at a glance that she would no longer refuse him any favors he might ask. To this letter of surrender he wrote her a response on September 11 which contained a note of restraint. He referred to his services in connection with Braddock's army:

Since I saw you I have been enabled to do some general services to the country and to the army for which both have thanked and praised me, and say they love me. They say so as you used to do; and if I were to ask any favours of them, they would perhaps as readily refuse me; so that I find little real advantage in being beloved, but it pleases my humour.

Now it is four months since I have been favoured with a single line from you; but I will not be angry with you, because it is my fault. I ran in debt to you three or four letters; and as I did not pay, you should not trust me any more, and you had some reason. . . . Though I should never make equal returns, you shall see I will keep fair accounts. Equal returns I can never make, though I should write to you by every post; for the pleasure I receive from

[31] Franklin, *Papers*, V, 535-537.

one of yours is more than you can have from two of mine. . . .

You have spun a long thread, five thousand and twenty-two yards. It will reach almost from Rhode Island hither. I wish I had hold of one end of it, to pull you to me. But you would break it rather than come. The cords of love and friendship are longer and stronger, and in times past have drawn me farther; even back from England to Philadelphia. I guess that some of the same kind will one day draw you out of that island.[32]

A month later, on October 16, 1755, Ben sent Catherine a letter which showed very clearly that caution was the line he was following and that sex was cowering in a corner. The tone of this missive is quite paternal: "I hear you are now in Boston, gay and lovely as usual. Let me give you some fatherly advice. . . . Be a good girl and don't forget your catechism. Go constantly to meeting, or church, till you get a good husband." [33]

From this letter Catherine could see that Ben wanted to blow out any sparks of affection he might have lighted in her heart. She did not see him again until 1763, after she had married William Greene and had had two children. Their final meeting was in 1776, when Catherine and her husband visited Franklin in Philadelphia.

On Catherine's part, their friendship could have culminated in passion and submission, but when this fact had become evident to Franklin he had hurriedly assumed the role of protector rather than lover. Still, Catherine Ray had lifted his eyes to distant horizons, intellectual and so-

[32] Quoted in Van Doren, *op. cit.*, pp. 237-239.
[33] Franklin, *Writings*, III, 288-289.

cial, where a series of public offices would require his best talents not only in America but at the courts of both England and France.

TO ENGLAND FOR THE
PENNSYLVANIA ASSEMBLY

Franklin's undoubted success with the *Gazette* and *Poor Richard's Almanack* brought him such a comfortable income that he decided to retire from some of his activities. In 1748 he made David Hall a partner in his enterprises and put him in charge of printing and the bookshop, while he continued to edit the *Gazette* and write the almanacs. The annual profits had amounted to £2000 a year. Franklin kept half this amount and turned the other half over to Hall, an arrangement that continued in effect until 1766.[34] It gave Franklin more leisure and left him with an income sufficient to meet all his needs.

In May, 1751, he sought appointment as deputy postmaster general of the colonies, and wrote to Peter Collinson in London with regard to it. After Elliot Benger, the postmaster general, died, Franklin and William Hunter of Williamsburg were appointed deputy postmasters general in August, 1753, but the salary was limited to £600 a year between them, "to be paid out of the money arising from the postage of letters." The two men worked in harmony, and Franklin suggested many improvements in the postal service. The receipts from the service increased rap-

[34] Fay, *op. cit.*, p. 216. See also William G. Roelker, ed., *Benjamin Franklin and Catherine Ray Greene: Their Correspondence, 1755-1790* (Phila., 1949).

idly under his able administration, and soon he enjoyed a rising income from that office.

But he had serious trouble on his hands in other quarters. In Philadelphia there was a constant quarrel between the Assembly and the governors appointed by the Penns. This friction became so heated that the Assembly finally decided to send Franklin to London to plead their cause. He arrived in the British capital on July 26, 1757, and his mission occupied five important years of his life. The quarrel between the Penns and the Assembly was finally settled through his efforts. The King in Council decided that the Assembly had the right to tax all the property in the Province with the exception of the unsurveyed wastelands of the Penn estate. Moreover, the Penns consented to cease their opposition to the circulation of a large amount of paper currency that had already been issued.

In London, Franklin was comfortably housed in the hospitable home of the charming Mrs. Margaret Stevenson at 7 Craven Street, by the Thames. She was most kind to him. She warmed his shirts before he put them on, and furnished him with long-sleeved nightgowns, flannel trousers, and comfortable slippers that induced pleasant sleep during the chilly London winters. He luxuriated in these pleasant surroundings so different from his cold quarters in Philadelphia.

Financially it would have been easy for him to pay the passage money for Deborah to come to London; but what would he have "done with his charming, subtle Mrs. Stevenson? How would his son William have supported Deborah? That would have been a problem indeed." [35]

There is no doubt that William, who was then very intent upon cutting a swath in London society, would have

[35] Fay, *op. cit.*, p. 292.

been very much opposed to Deborah's coming to London. Her obvious lack of culture would have greatly embarrassed him, and her mode of dress would have seemed dreadfully provincial to stylish Londoners.

In some ways William himself was a great worry to Franklin, who hoped that he would propose marriage to Marie Stevenson, the daughter of Franklin's landlady. William appeared to have accepted his father's viewpoint in this matter, but one morning he created consternation in the family circle by boldly presenting to Franklin an illegitimate grandson. Marie fled to the country, followed by letters from Franklin, who tried in vain to explain the situation.

This abrupt ending to the Marie-William idyl made continued residence at 7 Craven Street a little uncomfortable. Franklin now decided to return to Philadelphia. When he arrived there on November 1, 1762, he was met by a large crowd of friends, and the members of the Assembly were so pleased with his successful mission to London that they bestowed upon him a present of £3000.[36]

Franklin had been back in Philadelphia for only a short time when the quarrel between the Assembly and the Penns flared up again. He now realized that the old proprietary government had to go. At first he favored the conversion of Pennsylvania into a royal colony, but he soon perceived that the independence of the American colonies was inevitable and that popular government in Pennsylvania was the only workable remedy to cure the ills that had bedeviled that Province for decades. But this was a long glance into the future, and for a considerable time he turned away from reality and nursed dreams of an expanding British Empire.

[36] Fisher, *op. cit.*, p. 218.

In the meantime, the Assembly insisted that he return to London on a second mission; this one was to last a decade. When he reached London on December 11, 1764, he took up quarters once more in the pleasant home of Mrs. Stevenson. But he did not have much time for creature comforts. He was quickly drawn into the rising political currents that brought the passage of the Stamp Act in 1765. Franklin thought that the colonists would submit to this law without too much opposition, and recommended the appointment of John Hughes, a merchant of Philadelphia, as the distributor of the stamps. He soon realized his mistake, and voiced his opposition to the plans of the ministry for colonial taxation. This change of front brought him into high favor in the colonies, and he became the agent in London not only for Pennsylvania but also for New Jersey, Georgia, and Massachusetts.

But Ben could not be too strident in his opposition to the plans of the King and his ministers, for he was eager to secure a royal patent to vast unsurveyed lands along the American frontier. To this end he and a group of associates organized the Grand Ohio Company. The Lees of Virginia had organized the Mississippi Company seeking a grant of some of the same territory, and the competition of the two land companies was an important factor in the equation of bitterness between Franklin and Arthur Lee in Paris after 1776.[37]

[37] Thomas P. Abernethy, *Western Lands and the American Revolution* (New York, 1937), Chaps. I-VI. See also Clarence W. Alvord, *The Mississippi Valley in British Politics* (Cleveland, 1917, 2 vols.).

FRANKLIN GOES TO PARIS

Toward the end of his decade in England on his second mission, Franklin knew that Deborah was critically ill and desperately needed him, and several times he made preparations to return to Philadelphia and be with her in what he feared was her last illness. But hope of reconciliation with the mother country would not die; he refused to believe that a path to peace could not be found. In December, 1774, Deborah lost any desire to keep on living with Ben thousands of miles away.

Deborah had not been the answer to all his prayers, but she had been an inspiration that had given purpose to his early years in Philadelphia, and her boundless affection for him was like some Bethesda well that had been blessed by an angel of the Lord for his particular needs.

It was finally apparent to Franklin that he should no longer stay in London and wear out his heart on a task that he could never finish according to his ardent desires. On March 25, 1775, he embarked for Philadelphia with his beloved grandson William Temple, and when a favoring wind brought them into port on May 5, the first shots in the American Revolution had already been fired. He was soon elected to the Continental Congress, and then was made a member of the committee that framed the Declaration of Independence.

In London meanwhile, Arthur Lee was working to convince Louis XVI of the many advantages France would derive from extending secret military assistance to the struggling American colonies. Aided by the persuasive pen of Caron de Beaumarchais, he succeeded in winning royal assent to this assistance. Some six months later, on September 26, 1776, the Continental Congress appointed an official commission to go to France and supplement Arthur Lee's efforts. Besides Lee, the commission included Silas Deane and Benjamin Franklin. Franklin landed in France on December 3, 1776, and began a momentous mission. His important share in the treaty negotiations leading to peace with England has been told many times and does not need retelling here.[38] Nor do Franklin's shabby treatment of Arthur Lee, his failure to maintain any worthwhile system of bookkeeping relative to the millions of dollars that passed through his hands in Passy, and the fact that much of his ability to get shipments of military supplies from France was nullified by the actions of his secretary, Edward Bancroft, who turned out to be a traitor worse than Benedict Arnold.[39]

ELECTRICITY AND THE LADIES OF PARIS

In Paris Franklin made many mistakes and his record was marred by some inexcusable failures, but none of these occurred in his relations with women. In this regard he was a conspicuous success. As Bernard Fäy remarks:

He was adored from the highest ladies of the court to the lowest of chambermaids. Marie Antoinette had him explain the mysteries of physics to her, the Duchesse de Bourbon played chess with him, Madame Bertin, niece of

[38] Samuel F. Bemis, The *Diplomacy of the American Revolution* (New York, 1935), Chaps. XIV-XVIII.

[39] Burton J. Hendrick, *The Lees of Virginia* (Boston, 1935), Chaps. XI-XII; Abernethy, *op. cit.*, Chap. XIV; Fisher, *op. cit.*, pp. 290-297.

the Chancellor, took him for rides in her coach, the Comtesse Golofkin sang, "O God of Love!" for him, and they all wanted to kiss him and to call him "Papa.". . . . He could not appear in any salon but what he was immediately surrounded by several beauties, and if he sat down, they sat down too—on the arms of his chair.[40]

One of his favorites was Mademoiselle de Passy, daughter of the Comte de Boullainvilliers, who had a large chateau on the outskirts of Paris. Franklin was often a visitor to the chateau. He treasured her kisses, and she was so generous in her embraces that there were many sly remarks when she married the Comte de Tonnerre (Count of Thunder). He often faced the question: "How it is, Doctor Franklin, that with all your lightning rods you couldn't keep Thunder from hitting Mademoiselle de Passy?"

The French beauties he visited most frequently were Madame Helvétius and Madame Brillon de Jouy. In her youth Madame Helvétius had been outstandingly beautiful, and the years had been kind to her. Her family had an ancient background in Lorraine, but it was as poor as it was distinguished. Her education had been sadly neglected. Her range of knowledge was most limited; her writings would never have been approved by the French Academy, and her spelling would have shamed a scrubwoman. But her beauty had a dazzling quality that made men forget her academic deficiencies.

There had been a certain young man named Turgot who had an IQ that soared to dizzy heights and a future that appeared very inviting. But he had no particular fortune, and Mademoiselle de Ligniville, if she got married, would have no dowry. When Monsieur Turgot discovered

[40] Fäy, *op. cit.*, pp. 456-457.

this disturbing fact he became alarmed. As a budding philosopher and financier, he appraised the situation calmly. He was certain that he could have a comfortable future, but there was a possibility he would never reach it if he married a beauty whose only wealth was her exceptional good looks. So Monsieur Turgot and Mademoiselle de Ligniville swore eternal friendship, and she, after a decent interval, married Monsieur Helvétius, a famous financier who gratified her every whim and showed her the prevailing road to happiness.

When this road came to a sudden end with his demise, she still enjoyed a comfortable income, and she filled the vacuum caused by his death with eighteen cats, ten dogs, and a flock of assorted birds. The mess that resulted from this small zoo she conveniently overlooked, and Franklin's nose was not too particular.

Indeed, he was delighted to visit her country estate at Auteuil. When she entered her salon she would hold out a slender, bejeweled hand for him to kiss and then invite him to sit close to her and talk as only he could talk. At times he was serious, but he could charm her with his quick wit, which she realized was not real conversational food but which was certainly delicious spice. The peasant strain in him that had answered the brash call of Deborah warmed to the unrefined manners of Madame Helvétius, who did not bother to wash her face every day and whose salon, with all the attendant cats and dogs, had the mixed odors of a kennel.

A very graphic picture of Madame Helvétius and her relations with Franklin is given in a letter of Mrs. John Adams, who was none too favorably impressed with the free-and-easy manner of this French favorite:

She entered the room with a careless, jaunty air; upon seeing ladies who were strangers to her, she bawled out, 'Ah! mon Dieu, where is Franklin? Why did you not tell me there were ladies here?' You must suppose her speaking all this in French. 'How I look' said she, taking hold of a chemise made of tiffany, which she had on over a blue lute-string, and which looked as much upon the decay as her beauty, for she was once a handsome woman; her hair was frizzled; over it she had a small straw hat, with a dirty gauze half-handkerchief round it, and a bit of dirtier gauze than ever my maids wore was bowed on behind. She had a black gauze scarf thrown over her shoulders. She ran out of the room; when she returned, the Doctor entered at one door, she at the other; upon which she ran forward to him, caught him by the hand, 'Helas! Franklin;' then gave him a double kiss, one upon each cheek, and another one upon his forehead. When we went into the room to dine, she was placed between the Doctor and Mr. Adams. She carried on the chief of the conversation at dinner, frequently locking her hand into the Doctor's, and sometimes spreading her arms upon the backs of both the gentlemen's chairs, then throwing her arm carelessly upon the Doctor's neck.

I should have been greatly astonished at this conduct, if the good Doctor had not told me that in this lady I should see a genuine Frenchwoman, wholly free from affectation or stiffness of behavior, and one of the best women in the world. For this I must take the Doctor's word; but I should have set her down for a very bad one, although sixty years of age, and a widow. I own I was highly disgusted and never wish for an acquaintance with any ladies of this cast. After dinner she threw herself upon a settee, where she showed more than her feet. She had a little lapdog, who was, next to the Doctor, her favorite. This she kissed, and when he wet the floor, she wiped it up with her chemise. This is one of the Doctor's most intimate friends, with whom he dines once every week, and she with him. She is rich, and is my near neighbor; but I have not yet visited her. Thus you see, my dear, that manners differ exceedingly in different countries. I hope, however, to find amongst the French ladies manners more consistent with my ideas of decency, or I shall be a mere recluse.[41]

Franklin was in sharp disagreement with Mrs. Adams concerning Madame Helvétius. He had never been fastidious about untidiness in his home in Philadelphia when Deborah was in charge of the domestic scene, and his rooms at 7 Craven Street were often a scene of wild disorder, and Mrs. Stevenson was constantly busy picking up his clothes and keeping his papers in neat piles so he could consult them again. He felt at home in disorder.

Perhaps that was the reason he proposed marriage to Madame Helvétius on a day when he felt in high spirits. Such a surprising offer of marriage made her a little faint, and she reached for the mantelpiece for support. She pointed to a memorial of her late husband as an indication that she belonged to him even in death, but she kissed Franklin good-bye with unwonted tenderness.

After a sleepless night he wrote one of his fanciful essays which he took to her for calm reflection. It was entitled, "Descent to Hell." It described his own descent into Hell and his meeting there with Helvétius, who had lost no time in getting married again so that he could better stand the torments of Hell. It greatly surprised Franklin to see that his deceased wife, Deborah, was tied by a new marriage to Helvétius. When he chided her softly, she archly replied, "I was your wife for almost half a century;

[41] *Letters of Mrs. Adams, the Life of John Adams,* ed. C. F. Adams (Boston, 1841, 2 vols.), II, 55-56.

be content with that." Franklin then ended his fable with a pointed suggestion to Madame Helvétius: "Here I am. Let us have our revenge." [42]

She liked this turn of phrase, and her heart suddenly beat with a new tempo. She felt she must go consult with her old lover, Monsieur Turgot, now one of the King's ablest ministers. He immediately referred to the unpleasant fact that she was fifteen years closer to youth than Franklin, and that her friends would regard her as a little mad. She took a long ride in her carriage, away from her cats, dogs, and birds, with the fresh air cleansing her brain. Her decision was inevitable: she would not undertake another adventure in matrimony. When Franklin called to ask for her decision, she did not answer his question but heaped upon his plate a double serving of the thick whipped cream of which he was so fond. He knew the meaning of this generous gesture and so was spared the details of the sad story. His role as an ardent suitor was over.

But he had other roles with other women. At Auteuil he had dined once a week; at the home of Madame Brillon de Jouy he dined twice a week. She was not yet forty years of age, and Franklin thought she was beautiful. As a matter of fact, he had a good eye for beauty. As John Adams once wryly observed, "Franklin at the age of seventy-odd had neither lost his love of beauty nor his taste for it." [43] In the case of Madame Brillon de Jouy, much as in that of Madame Helvétius, her family had chosen a husband for her without consulting her wishes, and this husband was twenty-four years older than she. He had a consider-

[42] Fäy, *op. cit.*, p. 462.
[43] John Adams, *Works,* ed. C. F. Adams (Boston, 1850-1856, 10 vols.), III, 134.

able fortune so there was no difficulty in balancing the family budget, but intellectually he was not her equal, and he was lacking in many of the arts of refinement.

When he realized that his married life was not complete, he sought fulfillment in an intimate association with a tavern maid of twenty. Madame Brillon de Jouy sublimated her own desires in something spiritual, and her attitude toward Franklin was purely maternal. Ever the incurable optimist, he hoped she would tire of sublimation and be the warm woman she was made to be. But usually she wrote to him on a high level: "After your visit I could remember only your sensitive friendliness, your simplicity and goodness. I said to myself, this man is so good he will love me, and I have since begun to love you deeply, hoping you would return my affection." [44]

He soon returned her affection full measure, and at times, despite his age, he grew naughty and made advances. For this she gently reproved him: "People have the audacity to criticize my pleasant habit of sitting on your knee, and yours of always asking me for what I always refuse." She did not abandon this "pleasant habit," and Franklin kept asking the same old question and apparently receiving the same negative answer. It must have reminded him of the old game he had once played with Catherine Ray, but in that case when her heart softened his courage had fled. With Madame Brillon de Jouy he played the game for what it was worth, and some nights when she took a bath in a semicovered tub she would play chess with him until the wee hours of the morning. It is not recorded that he ever captured the queen.

There is a definite hint of sex in many of his letters to Madame Brillon de Jouy. In commenting upon an attack

[44] Franklin, *Writings*, X, 431.

of the gout, he slyly remarks, "When I was a young man and enjoyed more favours from the sex than at present, I never had the gout. If the ladies at Passy had more of that Christian charity which I have so often recommended to you, in vain, I would not have the gout now." [45] This gay note of badinage is continued in another letter from the lady. Franklin had remarked that if he were the Angel Gabriel he would like to carry her on his wings. In reply she made the following teasing comment:

> Your proposition to carry me on your wings, if you were the Angel Gabriel, made me laugh: but I would not accept it, though I am no longer very young nor a virgin. That Angel was a sly fellow, and your nature united to his would become too dangerous. I would be afraid of miracles happening; and miracles betwen women and angels might not always bring a redeemer.[46]

TWILIGHT OF THE GODS

As the summer of 1784 approached, Franklin felt that his mission in Paris had been completed, and so he prepared to return to Philadelphia. He sailed from Le Havre on July 22 and arrived home on September 13. The ocean voyage had greatly benefited his health, so that when the federal convention met in Philadelphia in May, 1787, he became a member of the delegation from Pennsylvania. His contributions to the work of the convention were minor, but on June 28 he put forth a suggestion that surprised the members, one that would immediately have been outlawed by the present Supreme Court of the United States. Turning to George Washington, who presided over the

[45] *Ibid.*, X, 414-415.
[46] *Ibid.*, X, 424-425.

sessions of the convention, he made this moving, dramatic plea:

> How has it happened, Sir, that we have not hitherto once thought of humbly applying to the Father of lights to illuminate our understandings? . . . I have lived, Sir, a long time, and the longer I live the more convincing proofs I see of this truth: that God governs in the affairs of men. And if a sparrow cannot fall to the ground without His notice, is it probable that an empire can rise without His aid? . . . I believe that without His concurring aid we shall succeed in this political building no better than the builders of Babel. We shall be divided by our little partial local interests; our projects will be confounded; and we ourselves shall become a reproach and byword to future ages.[47]

After the sessions of the federal convention terminated on September 17, 1787, Franklin took a brief rest and then began the publication of some pamphlets. His active mind kept pushing a laggard body until he felt completely exhausted, and he realized that the shadows of night were fast closing in around him. In the last months of 1789 he became increasingly weak and pain-wracked, and he began to look forward to an early deliverance. On the afternoon of April 17, 1790, he asked his daughter for fresh sheets for his bed so that he could "die in a decent manner." Beside his bed were his grandsons, Temple Franklin and Benny Bache. They heard him murmur faintly: "A dying man can do nothing easy." He convulsively seized Benny's hand and then, with a deep sigh, closed his eyes. He was already seeking the familiar form of Deborah.

[47] Max Farrand, *Records of the Federal Convention* (New York, 1911, 6 vols.), I, 451-452.

three

Thomas Jefferson
[1743-1826]

REBECCA BURWELL

Anyone who has visited Monticello realizes that Jefferson had a sharp eye for alluring lines and arresting curves. At times he was particularly interested in feminine architecture. He had an artist's appreciation of the glory that was Greece which was not confined to the cold sculptures of Phidias. He was always aware of the attraction of a well-turned ankle, a prettily rounded breast, or a soft, inviting voice that set one's nerves on urge. In other words, Jefferson was not only a philosopher.

In Virginia in colonial days the door of a young man's heart was always eager to open at some soft feminine touch. Jefferson's heart had this common characteristic, and while he was still in his teens he learned a few things about the way of a maid with a man. But at nineteen he had not completely passed out of the age of innocence, and his letters to his intimate friend John Page betray a naïveté that is refreshing. Page was the son of Mann Page of Rosewell who owned a princely estate in Gloucester County. On Christmas Day, 1762, while visiting Lewis Burwell at Fairfield, the ancient seat of the Burwell family, Jefferson wrote a long letter to Page in the seriocomic style that he affected at that time. The Burwell home was badly in need of repair, and the roof over the bedroom in which Jefferson slept had many leaks. This fact explains some references in the letter.

I am sure if there is such a thing as a Devil in this world, he must have been here last night and have had some hand in contriving what happened to me. . . . You know it rained last night. When I went to bed, I laid my watch in the usual place, and going to take her up after I arose this morning, I found her in the same place, it's true, but all afloat in water, let in at a leak in the roof of the house. Now you know, there were a thousand other spots where it might have chanced to leak as well as this one. It's my opinion that the Devil came and bored a hole over it on purpose. . . .

Well, as I was saying, my poor watch had lost her speech. I should not have cared much for this, but something worse attended it; the subtle particles of the water with which the case was filled had, by their penetration, so overcome the cohesion of the particles of the paper, of which my dear picture and watch paper were composed, that in attempting to take them out to dry them, good God! my cursed fingers gave them such a rent, as I fear

I never shall get over. And now, although the picture may
be defaced, there is so lively an image of her imprinted
in my mind, that I shall think of her too often, I fear, for
my peace of mind.[1]

The "dear picture" which Jefferson was carrying in his
watch was of Rebecca Burwell, the sister of his host and
the Belinda of some of his early letters. Her father had
died earlier in 1762, and Rebecca had gone to live with
her aunt, Elizabeth Burwell, who had married William
Nelson, a wealthy planter of Yorktown. As a member of
the Council, Nelson often stayed in Williamsburg with his
family, and it was during one of these visits that Jefferson
danced with Rebecca in the famous Appolo Room of the
Raleigh Tavern.

She was only sixteen at the time of Jefferson's letter to
Page, and there is no painting or exact description of her.
Jefferson stresses her "goodness" and that feminine quality
which attracted his attention. He had no doubt that her
"image" would be permanently "imprinted" on his mind.
At any rate, on January 20, 1763, he once more wrote to
Page and referred to a familiar topic. It is apparent that he
now had a rival for Rebecca's affections, and he asked
Page what he should do under the circumstances:

How does R[ebecca] B[urwell] do? Had I better stay
here and do nothing, or go down and do less? Inclination
tells me to go, receive my sentence, and be no longer in
suspence: but, reason says if you go and your attempt
proves unsuccessful you will be ten times more wretched
than ever. I verily believe Page that I shall die soon, and

[1] Thomas Jefferson, *Papers,* ed. Julian P. Boyd (Princeton, 1950-
1961, 16 vols.), I, 3-4.

yet I can give no other reason for it but that I am tired with living.[2]

But life kept merrily on despite Jefferson's professed desire to die, and his thoughts began to range to distant travel. This, of course, would seriously conflict with any ideas of matrimony. This angle of the situation would have to be kept from the knowledge of Rebecca's guardian, who might seriously object to any plans for marriage at a very indefinite date:

> No, no, Page, whatever assurances I may give her in private of my esteem for her, or whatever assurances I may ask in return from her, depend on it they must be kept in private. Necessity will oblige me to proceed in a method which is not generally thought fair, that of treating with a ward before obtaining the approbation of her guardian. . . . If I am to succeed the sooner I know it the less uneasiness I shall have to go through. If Belinda will not accept of my service it shall not be offered to another. I should be scared to death at making her so unreasonable [a proposal] as that of waiting untill I returned from Britain. . . . But the event at last must be this, that if she consents, I shall be happy; if she does not, I must endeavor to be as much so as possible.[3]

Feeling he must confront Rebecca and make her a formal proposal of marriage, young Jefferson rehearsed his approach carefully and memorized appropriate expressions of affection. But when his opportunity came on the evening of October 6, 1763, in the Appolo Room of the Raleigh Tavern, he became a tonguetied schoolboy and for-

[2] *Ibid.*, I, 9-11.
[3] *Ibid.*, I, pp. 11-12.

got all the gold-laced phrases he had hoped would serve
as keys to Rebecca's heart. His utter confusion and faint
heart he described in a letter to Page the following day:

> In the most melancholy fit that ever any poor soul was,
> I sit down to write to you. Last night, as merry as agree-
> able company and dancing with Belinda in the Appolo
> could make me, I never could have thought the succeed-
> ing sun would have seen me so wretched as I now am!
> I was prepared to say a great deal: I had dressed up in
> my own mind, such thoughts as occurred to me, in as mov-
> ing language as I knew how, and expected to have per-
> formed in a tolerably creditable manner. But good God!
> When I had an opportunity of venting them, a few broken
> sentences uttered in great disorder, and interrupted with
> pauses of uncommon length, were the too visible marks of
> my strange confusion! For God's sake come.[4]

Jefferson soon realized that he did not need John Page
to serve as a love counselor. Slowly his fevered pulses returned to normal, and he felt that his head and not his
heart was in control of his actions. He sought out Rebecca
Burwell and laid the situation before her in a most reasonable manner. He pointed out to her that before she could
get a wedlock upon him he was determined to take an
extended trip to England. This would consume considerable time, and it was therefore impossible for him to fix
any date when he would be ready for matrimony. She
should not entertain the slightest doubt, of course, about
the constancy and purity of his devotions to her. The story
is best told in Jefferson's own words. In a letter to John
Page dated January 19, 1764, he remarks:

[4] *Ibid.*, I, 11-12.

I told you our confab in the Appolo: but I believe
I never told you that we had another occasion. I then
opened my mind more freely and fully. I mentioned the
necessity of my going to England, and the delays which
would consequently be occasioned by that. I said in what
manner I should conduct myself till then and explained
my reasons, which appeared to give that satisfaction I
could have wished. In short I managed in such a manner
that I was tolerably easy myself without doing anything
which could give Rebecca's friends the least umbrage,
were the whole that passed to be related to them.[5]

It was obvious to Rebecca that in Jefferson's courtship
of her, caution had replaced ardor. She quickly made other
marital plans, and on May 24, 1764, she and Jacquelin
Ambler were married. Jefferson was now free to spend his
time in pursuit of the law rather than of fair ladies, and his
years under the wise tutelage of George Wythe made
him an outstanding legal scholar.

BETSY WALKER

There is no doubt that Jefferson profited by his study
under Chancellor Wythe, but his eyes were not always
upon his law books. In June, 1764, Jefferson's intimate
friend John Walker married Elizabeth Moore, the viva-
cious and attractive daughter of Bernard Moore of Chel-
sea, King William County. Shortly after his marriage,
Walker went to Fort Stanwix to serve as secretary to the
Virginia commissioners who were attempting to negotiate
a treaty with the Indians. He left his pretty wife under
the care of Jefferson, who seemed to think that he should

[5] *Ibid.*, I, 13-14.

serve as a substitute husband. The wife had other ideas, and according to her story she repulsed young Tom's amorous advances. When Walker returned from Fort Stanwix, his relations with Jefferson remained friendly and many letters were exchanged between them. Jefferson left in 1784 on his mission to France, and only then did Walker's wife finally tell her husband that in 1768 and in subsequent years Jefferson had made improper advances toward her. In a much later letter to General Henry Lee (March 28, 1805), Walker made this statement:

In '68 I was called to Fort Stanwix, being secretary, or a clerk to the Virginia commissioners at the treaty with the Indians there. . . . I left my wife and infant daughter at home, relying on Mr. Jefferson as my neighbor and fast friend. . . . I returned in November, having been absent more than four months. During my absence Mr. Jefferson's conduct to Mrs. Walker was improper, so much so as to have laid the foundation of her constant objection to my leaving Mr. Jefferson my executor, telling me that she wondered why I could place such confidence in him.

At Shadwell, his own house, in '69 or '70, on a visit common to us being neighbors he renewed his caresses, placed in Mrs. Walker's gown sleeve cuff, a paper tending to convince her of the innocence of promiscuous love. This, Mrs. Walker, on the first glance, tore to pieces. After this we went on a visit to Col. Coles, a mutual acquaintance and distant neighbor. Mr. Jefferson was there. On the ladys retiring to bed, he pretended to be sick, complained of a headache and left the gentlemen, among whom I was. Instead of going to bed, as his sickness authorized belief, he stole into my room where my wife was undressing or in bed. He was repulsed with indignation and menaces of alarm, and stole off.

In '71 Mr. Jefferson was married and yet continued his

efforts to destroy my peace until the latter end of the
year '79. One particular instance I remember. My old
house had a passage upstairs with a room on each side
and opposite doors. Mr. Jefferson and his wife slept in
one. I and my wife in the other. At the end of the passage was a small room used by my wife as her private
apartment. She visited it early and later. Mr. Jefferson,
knowing her custom, was found in his shirt ready to seize
her on her way from her chamber—indecent in manner.
In '83 Mr. Jefferson went to France. His wife died pre-
viously. From '79 Mr. Jefferson desisted in his attempts on
my peace.[6]

Jefferson's most scholarly biographer, Dumas Malone,
discusses this episode as follows:

It was in the year he was twenty-five that Jefferson
made a mistake. He was then unmarried. Full of physical strength and vigor, and for four months his friend
was away from home. . . . A generation afterwards John
[Walker] said that during his absence Jefferson's conduct
towards Mrs. Walker was improper. . . . It was not until
after he [Jefferson] had gone to France in 1784 that Mrs.
Walker told her husband about Jefferson's designs on her.
As Walker wrote it down fifteen or twenty years after he
got the report, it was a disgusting tale which bore marks
of gross and willful exaggeration, whatever may have
been the cause. In the absence of other testimony, such
an incredible story cannot be accepted in detail.[7]

[6] The original of this statement was probably enclosed in Walker's
letter on March 28, 1805, to General Henry Lee, DLC (document, library of Congress) 148:25833. See also DLC 155:27117-27, 121.

[7] Dumas Malone, *Jefferson, the Virginian,* Vol. I of *Jefferson and
His Time* (Boston, 1948), pp. 154-155.

It is probable that the story about Jefferson and Mrs. Walker would never have been published except for the extreme partisan bitterness that existed toward Jefferson after his inauguration as President. The first open breach between Walker and Jefferson may have been caused by the election in Virginia of James Monroe to the United States Senate in 1790; Walker had been one of the contestants for this important federal office. In any event, even before the inauguration of Jefferson as President, the story about Jefferson and Mrs. Walker had been given some currency, and in 1802 the notorious scandalmonger James Thomson Callender published it far and wide. He added a variation concerning Jefferson's conduct with one of his attractive slave women.[8] It was not long before these scurrilous stories were circulated in New England and precipitated a debate in the House of Representatives of Massachusetts.[9]

In response to all these charges Jefferson made a reply in a letter to a friend, Secretary of the Navy Robert Smith, on July 1, 1805: "You will perceive that I plead guilty to one of their charges, that when young and single I offered love to a handsome lady. I acknowledge its incorrectness. It is the only one founded in truth among all their allegations against me." [10]

If he had pressed his affections upon Rebecca Burwell with half the ardor he allegedly lavished upon Betsy Walker, she would probably never have married Jacquelin Ambler. If one puts any credence in the Walker narrative, it would appear that Jefferson continued his designs upon

---

[8] *Richmond Recorder,* October 27, 1802.

[9] *New England Palladium,* January 18, 1805.

[10] Thomas Jefferson, *Correspondence,* with notes by W. C. Ford (Boston, 1916), p. 115.

Betsy even after his marriage. But when one considers the deep affection which Jefferson showed for his wife in every way, it hardly seems possible that during their decade of complete happiness he could have entertained any fugitive fancy for another woman.

MARTHA SKELTON

As early as October, 1770, Jefferson was strongly attracted to Martha Skelton. She was the daughter of John Wayles of Charles City County, who had a plantation known as The Forest. In November, 1766, at the age of seventeen, she had married Bathurst Skelton, who had been a student at William and Mary College and had known Jefferson and his circle of friends. After scarcely two years of marriage, Bathurst Skelton suddenly died, in September, 1768, and it was not long before Martha's beauty caught Jefferson's fancy.

When one has seen the portrait of Sally Fairfax, it is easy to understand George Washington's infatuation with her. But there is no portrait of Martha Skelton, and no detailed contemporary description of her exists. Jefferson's biographer Henry S. Randall had a fertile imagination and had no difficulty in supplying a pen portrait of her appearance at the time of her marriage to Jefferson: "Mrs. Skelton . . . was distinguished for her beauty, her accomplishments, and her solid merit. In person, she was a little above medium height, slightly but exquisitely formed. Her complexion was brilliant—her large, expressive eyes of the richest shade of hazel—her luxuriant hair of the finest tinge of auburn." [11]

[11] Henry S. Randall, *Life of Thomas Jefferson* (New York, 1858, 3 vols.), I, 63.

Mr. Randall was probably on firm ground when he remarked that Mrs. Skelton "walked, rode, and danced with admirable grace and spirit—sang, and played the spinet and harpsichord with uncommon skill. She was also well read and intelligent; conversed agreeably; possessed excellent sense and a lively play of fancy; and had a frank, warm-hearted, and somewhat impulsive disposition." [12]

It was her lively playing on the harpsichord that particularly attracted Jefferson's attention, and he realized that at her home he could indulge his passion for playing the violin. He quickly discovered that his voice blended pleasantly with hers, and their duets were exercises in harmony that produced a spirit of togetherness. One night two rivals of Jefferson for Martha's hand were ushered into a large living room at the Forest, and after being seated they heard from the adjoining room the soft strains of Jefferson's violin with the accompanying notes of the harpsichord. The duet of Martha's and Thomas' voices made such a chord of sweet harmony that Jefferson's rivals followed the practice of the well-known Arabs of story and song, and "silently stole away."

Just how soon Jefferson developed a serious interest in Martha after Bathurst's death is not known, but following a formal call at The Forest in October, 1770, he became a regular visitor. By the Christmas holidays he knew he was in love with Martha and began thinking in terms of marriage. Apparently there was temporary parental objection. In a letter to James Ogilvie on February 20, 1771, Jefferson comments upon the difficulties of a friend who wishes to get married but is hindered by "the unfeeling temper of a parent who delays, perhaps refuses to approve her daughter's choice." Jefferson was up against similar ob-

[12] *Ibid.*, I, 63-64.

jections: "I too am in that way; and have still greater difficulties to encounter not from the frowardness of parents, nor perhaps want of feeling in the fair one, but from other causes as unpliable to my wishes as these." [13]

As his visits to the Forest became more frequent, he suddenly conceived the idea of improving the quality of the duets he and Mrs. Skelton played. After their marriage they would continue their duets at the home he was building at Monticello. In anticipation of these blissful days, he wrote Thomas Adams in London on June 1 and ordered a fine "forte-piano." "Send me this instrument then instead of the Clavichord," he ordered, "and let the case be of fine mahogany, solid, not vineered. The compass from Double G to F. in alt. and plenty of spare strings: and the workmanship of the whole very handsome, and worthy [of] the acceptance of a lady for whom I intend it." [14]

On August 3 Jefferson wrote Robert Skipwith and requested him to "offer prayers for me too at that shrine to which tho' absent, I pray continual devotions. In every scheme of happiness she is placed in the foreground of the picture, as the principal figure. Take that away and it is no picture for me." [15]

In the last months of 1771 it was evident that the marriage of Martha and Thomas would take place in the near future. In December Jefferson noted in his account book the amount he paid for curtains for Monticello, and finally he recorded the price of a bed. The wedding was celebrated at The Forest on New Year's Day, 1772. The bride was twenty-three and the groom was approaching thirty.

[13] Jefferson, *Papers,* I, 62-64.
[14] *Ibid.,* I, 71-72.
[15] *Ibid.,* I, 76-78.

The festivities lasted more than two weeks, and finally on January 18 Jefferson and his bride began their long drive to Monticello. At first they faced a light snow but it steadily grew heavier, and finally they had to abandon their light phaeton and proceed on horseback. They stopped for a short while at Blenheim, one of the plantations owned by Colonel Edward Carter, and at sunset moved on to Monticello through snow that had reached a depth of two feet.

It was late at night when Monticello came in sight. They stopped at one of the outbuildings that had recently been completed. The fires were out and the servants had retired to their quarters. But the happy couple had their love to keep them warm, and high spirits were maintained at a proper pitch from a highly prized bottle found on a shelf behind some books.[16]

When spring finally broke through at Monticello, Jefferson and Martha paid a lengthy visit to Williamsburg, where they saw their many friends and enjoyed the theater. At the end of May they went to The Forest for a month and returned to Monticello during the first week in July. On September 27, 1772, their first child was born, a daughter, named Martha after her mother. Jefferson called her Patsy, and she was a delight to him during his long life.

In May, 1773, deep shadows fell upon Monticello. On May 16 Jefferson's brother-in-law, Dabney Carr, suddenly died of "bilious fever," and was buried at Monticello. On Carr's tombstone Jefferson wrote an epitaph: "Thomas Jefferson, who of all men living, loved him most." He showed the greatest solicitude for his widowed sister and her six children, and cared for little Peter Carr as he would have done for his own son.

[16] See Randall, *op. cit.*, I, 64-65.

Scarcely had Dabney Carr's sad rites been carried out when the news came of the death of John Wayles, Martha Jefferson's father. Fortunately, his children were grown and were amply provided for. According to Dumas Malone, the immediate effect of Martha's inheritance was the "more than doubling" of the "ease of circumstances" at Monticello. For example, Mrs. Jefferson came into possession of at least 135 slaves alone. These "servants," as Jefferson called them, were devoted to him and "made his home life comfortable and jolly." [17]

A picture of Jefferson's home life at Monticello is given by the French traveler, the Marquis de Chastellux:

Let me describe to you a man, not yet forty, tall and with a mild and pleasant countenance, but whose mind and understanding are ample substitutes for every exterior grace. An American, who without ever having quitted his country, is at once a musician, skilled in drawing; a geometrician, an astronomer, a natural philosopher, legislator and statesman. A senator of America who sat for two years in the famous Congress which brought about the revolution. . . . A mild and amiable wife, charming children of whose education he himself takes charge, a house to embellish, great provisions to improve, and the arts and sciences to cultivate; these are what remain to Mr. Jefferson after having played a principal character in the theatre of the New World.[18]

But this pleasant domestic scene was soon to be disturbed by rumors of war; and in May, 1765, Jefferson

[17] Malone, *op. cit.*, I, 163.

[18] Marquis de Chastellux, *Travels in North America* (Dublin, 1787, 2 vols.), II, 42-43. For Jefferson's life at Monticello, see Sarah N. Randolph, *The Domestic Life of Thomas Jefferson* (Cambridge, 1939).

heard Patrick Henry make his famous incendiary speech that lighted the torch of revolution. As a member of the House of Burgesses, Jefferson's time was taken up more and more by affairs of state, and his absences from Monticello became more frequent and prolonged. In 1774 he drafted some resolutions which he hoped would be used as instructions to the Virginia delegation that was to be sent to the first Continental Congress. Without his knowledge they were printed in pamphlet form in Williamsburg under the title *A Summary View of the Rights of British America.*[19]

Before the end of the year the pamphlet was reprinted in Philadelphia and twice in England.[20] It added considerable prestige to Jefferson's name as a bold and learned champion of colonial rights. As Jefferson himself later remarked, "If it had any merit, it was that of first taking our true ground, and that which was afterwards assumed and maintained."[21] *The Summary View* attracted attention throughout colonial America, and it was inevitable that Jefferson would be sent to the Continental Congress to replace Peyton Randolph, who had returned to Williamsburg to preside over the fevered meetings of the House of Burgesses.

In Virginia Lord Dunmore greeted the year 1776 by putting Norfolk to the torch, and thus the revolutionary movement had a fiery start. Fortunately, Monticello was not affected by Lord Dunmore's antics. During the early months of 1776 Jefferson stayed at home and closely watched the tide of revolution rapidly rise. He was in

[19] Jefferson, *Papers*, I, 121-137.
[20] Thomas Jefferson, *Writings*, ed. Paul L. Ford (New York, 1892-1899, 10 vols.), I, 421-447.
[21] Jefferson, *Papers*, IX, 258.

agreement with Richard Henry Lee, who expressed the popular sentiment that a person might as well "expect to wash an Ethiopian white, as to remove the taint of despotism from the British court." [22]

In Philadelphia the members of the Continental Congress, familiar with Jefferson's *Summary View,* turned at once to Jefferson when a committee was appointed in June, 1776, to draft a Declaration of Independence.[23] After drafting the historic document Jefferson went to Williamsburg, where in October, 1776, he took his seat in the House of Delegates. The next three years, until he assumed the duties of governor of Virginia in June, 1779, he regarded as the most creative period in his life. There is no doubt that his work on the revision of the laws of the state was most fruitful and ushered in a profound change in the economic and social structure of the state. As governor he combed Virginia bare of troops and supplies and sent them south in order to keep the faltering revolutionary movement alive in the Carolinas. The British military retaliated by sending raiding parties far and wide in Virginia in 1780, and chased Jefferson and his family away from Monticello.

As a result of these British raids, charges of misconduct were preferred against Jefferson in the House of Delegates. After he presented his answers to these charges, a resolution was unanimously adopted in both the Senate and the House of Delegates that the General Assembly wished "in the strongest manner, to declare the high opinion which they entertain of Mr. Jefferson's ability,

[22] Richard Henry Lee, *Letters,* ed. (New York, 1911-1914, 2 vols.), I, 173.

[23] See Carl L. Becker, *The Declaration of Independence* (New York, 1940).

rectitude, and integrity, as Chief Magistrate of this Commonwealth." [24]

When he returned to Monticello in June, 1781, his family consisted of two daughters—Martha, who was in her tenth year, and Polly, in her third. Soon there would be another daughter, Lucy Elizabeth. Jefferson had absorbed into the Monticello group his sister Martha with her six offspring and his days were kept busy teaching these nine children and running the plantation.

Jefferson was particularly happy to have his sister with him because he had grave fears concerning his wife's health after bearing another child. On May 6, 1782, two days before his last child was born, he wrote to the speaker of the House of Delegates, John Tyler, declining the office of delegate to which he had recently been elected.[25] Tyler did not realize the gravity of Mrs. Jefferson's condition, and impressed with the need of Jefferson's services he wrote to Monticello on May 16 as follows: "At this time when the Republic wants to be organized and requires your influence to promote this desirable end, I can not but think the House may insist upon you to give attendance without incurring the censure of being rigid." [26]

To his intimate friend James Monroe, Jefferson wrote a long letter on May 20, and then for some months his friends heard nothing more from him. In his letter to Monroe he endeavored to make it clear that he no longer entertained any "political ambition." His long service in public affairs had caused him to neglect the situation at

[24] *The Statutes at Large, Being a Collection of All the Laws of Virginia,* ed. W. W. Hening (Richmond, 1809-1823, 13 vols.) X, 568-569.
[25] LC 8:1232.
[26] LC 8:1235-1236.

Monticello, and his "private affairs" had run into "great disorder and ruin." In summing up his reasons for declining to serve in the House of Delegates, he referred to the unjust way he had been treated by the members of that body, before whom he had stood "arraigned for treason of the heart and not merely weakness of the head." [27] Madison, who was not familiar with the situation at Monticello, wrote to Edmund Randolph on June 11: "The mode in which he seems determined to revenge the wrong received from his country does not appear to me to be dictated either by Philosophy or patriotism." [28]

As Mrs. Jefferson's condition grew more critical, Jefferson became almost frantic with grief, and when the end came on September 6, 1782, he was led from the room nearly insensible. For three weeks he remained in his room, and then he began a period of incessant riding, at times at such breakneck speed that his sisters greatly feared an accident. By mid-October he slowly emerged from a "stupor of mind" which had caused him to be "as dead to the world as she was whose loss occasioned it." [29]

Jefferson's affection for Martha was as deep as it was exclusive. She belonged to him alone, and there are no sprightly letters from Martha to her many friends in the Jefferson collection. If such existed, he destroyed them. So it was with regard to the letters that passed between him and Martha. The intimacies of a dearly beloved wife and her husband he was determined to keep inviolate. He saw to it that no mementos of hers were preserved for posterity. There are many relics of the Jefferson family, but none

---

[27] Jefferson, *Writings*, III, 56-60.
[28] James Madison, *Writings*, ed. Gaillard Hunt (New York, 1900-1910, 9 vols.), I, 207-208.
[29] Randall, *op. cit.*, I, 382.

of Martha—not one ringlet of her hair, not a garment she may have worn, not a piece of jewelry she may have prized. She had borne him six children in ten years, and her love for him had been her undoing. She had not reached the age of thirty-four when she died.

After Martha's death Jefferson sought solace in an appointment that would take him away from Monticello. In the fall of 1782 Madison moved in Congress for a renewal of Jefferson's appointment as a member of the American commission to negotiate a peace with England. Madison's motion was promptly accepted by Congress, and Jefferson was glad to accept the new appointment. But there were many delays over the matter of an acceptable sailing ship for his trip, and finally Congress informed him that a treaty of peace had been signed and he was not needed abroad.

Then in June, 1783, he received word of his election as one of Virginia's delegates to the Continental Congress. He served in that body for six months, during which period he drafted no fewer than thirty-one state papers, including the well-known Ordinance of 1784. On May 7, 1784, he was elected by Congress as a minister plenipotentiary to share in negotiating treaties of amity and commerce with European nations, and on July 5 he sailed from Boston on the good ship *Ceres*. Soon, much to his surprise, the strings of his heart suddenly resumed the vibrations they had not experienced since Rebecca Burwell had softly played upon them in the Appolo Room of the Raleigh Tavern so many years before. Upon this occasion they were artfully caressed in Paris by Maria Cosway, who knew all the notes in the melody of love.

MARIA COSWAY

Before Jefferson met Maria Cosway, he discharged some important official duties. He and his oldest daughter, Martha, landed in France on July 31 and went immediately to Paris, where his first task was to place Martha in a select convent school. He then sent for a stay-maker, a mantua-maker, a milliner, a shoemaker, and a *friseur*. When Martha was finally fitted out in the proper crimson uniform and formally entered in the convent school, Jefferson prepared himself for court. The Continental Congress had decided to appoint him minister to France, and it was up to him to see that at least in the matter of sartorial splendor he would be a worthy successor to Benjamin Franklin. He engaged the services of a *valet de chambre,* a *pédicure,* a *tailleur,* and a barber. He then purchased knee breeches, lace ruffles, silk stockings, embroidered waistcoats, an umbrella cane, and visiting cards.[30]

When he paid his respects to the French foreign minister, his dress was impeccable and his wit sharp. To Count Vergennes's question of whether he had come from America to replace "le Docteur Franklin," he quickly replied, "No one can *replace* him, sir. I am only his *successor.*"

Paris soon learned that Jefferson not only spoke fluent French but was as versatile as the many-sided Franklin. He handled his official duties with easy competence and had time for diversions in his leisure hours. There were subscriptions for seats in the Tuileries and tickets to the opera, the Italian theater, the French comedy, and an oc-

[30] Helen D. Bullock, *My Head and My Heart* (New York, 1945), pp. 6-7.

casional *concert spirituel*. French society extended him a warm welcome. He would enter into learned arguments with the Comte de Buffon, the eminent zoologist; he amazed Madame de Tessé with his wide-ranging knowledge of botany and presented her with an excellent collection of native Virginia seeds. In the field of political theory he had frequent discussions with eminent scholars like Condorcet, Du Pont de Nemours, La Rochefoucauld, and Chastellux. In order properly to entertain such a brilliant company, he rented the elegant house of the Comte de Langeac on the corner of the Champs Élysées and the Rue Neuve de Berry.

One of his American friends who came to visit him in this grand American legation was John Trumbull, the famous artist. He requested Jefferson to accompany him on a visit to his friends and fellow artists, Richard and Maria Cosway. Cosway was an eminently successful portrait painter, and his miniatures were famous all over the Continent. In 1786 he had come to Paris to paint the portraits of the family of the Duc d'Orléans.

Maria has also achieved distinction as a painter and had exhibited her work at the Royal Academy. As a musician she gave entertainments that attracted the social elite of several European capitals. She was seventeen years younger than her foppish husband, who was called by some critics Tiny Cosmetic. Maria had been born in Florence, Italy, where her father, Charles Hadfield, had had a large hostelry much frequented by English nobility and gentry. She had been brought up in a famous convent, and when her father died her ambitious mother had taken her back to London in search of a rich suitor. Before long she was married to Richard Cosway, whose portraits and miniatures were quite the rage. The Cosway residence at 20

Stratford Place became a focal point where fashionable and wealthy Londoners went for entertainment. William Parsons, the composer, was often present, and Sir Joshua Reynolds was attracted by the evident talents of Maria, who in 1778 at the age of nineteen had been elected to the Academy of Fine Arts in Florence.

It was inevitable that a young lady with an excess of beauty, talent, and charm should have many admirers, and it was whispered that the Prince of Wales was a member of this group. Some loose tongues also said that Maria had once accompanied the Italian singer Luigi Marchesi on a trip to the Continent. It was not believed that Maria took this trip to improve her accent.

At any rate, the September day in 1786 that Trumbull introduced Jefferson to Maria Cosway was one he would never forget. Rebecca Burwell had adorned Williamsburg society when he had been a callow youth in college, and Betsy Walker had seemed like Temptation written with a capital T when the fires of his youth burned through the barriers of restraint. Then for a decade Martha Skelton had led him down the road to happiness in a quiet and unobtrusive manner. He had never met a woman like Maria Cosway.

Her beauty was so breathtaking that he felt compelled to borrow a line from a famous poet and ask a question that demanded a quick answer: "Maria Cosway and beauty, which of you copied the other?" But she had more than extraordinary beauty. Her voice was soft and alluring, and at times it took on overtones that set him all atremble. When her fingers stroked the strings of a harp he felt at once that the notes had a strange haunting quality, like the sound of some spirit lute touched on some spirit sea. Her masses of golden curls were caught up in a coiffure that made his fingers twitch with longing as he held them back from a gesture of warm affection. Her large blue eyes were bright mirrors in which he could see all the earthly joys his heart desired and all the warning signs his cool brain had hastily erected along his road of vision. He was charmed by her blithe spirit and her gay conversation, which might drift into several different languages when she anxiously sought to find the words that best expressed her lively sentiments.

In order to lengthen his hours with Maria, Jefferson hurriedly dispatched to the Duchesse de la Rochefoucauld d'Anville a dubious note informing her that because of urgent official business he could not dine with her that evening. This same official business kept him busy on many subsequent days when he and Maria explored the sights of Paris. Often his carriage would stop at Maria's residence in the Rue Coq-Héron, and they would "hie away" to the Bois de Boulogne, Saint-Cloud, Marly, and other points of interest near the beautiful French capital. At the end of a glorious day he would gaily remark, "What a mass of happiness have we travelled over!" But his cautious mind often whispered to his wayward heart, "I reminded you of the follies of the first day."

Lovers seldom listen to such counsels of perfection. While Mr. Cosway painted his pictures, Jefferson and Maria continued their rounds of delight. He was fully aware of her charms and alluded to her "modesty, beauty, and that softness of disposition which is the ornament of her sex and the charm of ours." They were particularly fond of the lovely vistas in the park of Saint-Cloud, where gleaming cascades of water linked the marble fountains with a chain of fluent silver to the slow-moving Seine.

That September was a month that always lived brightly

in Jefferson's memory. He and Maria drove through the wooded hills that bordered the Seine, toward Saint-Germain-en-Laye. From the broad terrace they could see the spires of distant Paris and follow the course of the Seine, running like a bright thread through the green tapestry of the French countryside. From Saint-Germain-en-Laye they slowly made their way to Marly, the favorite retreat of Louis XIV. They lovingly inspected the superb, carefully ordered gardens with the leisure that attends the movements of persons who fondly hope that the big moments of life can be stretched into hours.

The last of these romantic sightseeing tours took place when they visited the Desert de Retz, a new *anglo-chinois* garden some four miles from Saint-Germain-en-Laye. Among other buildings was an exquisite Temple to the God Pan. The clear call from the pipes of Pan never left the sensitive ears of Jefferson, who looked back upon this tour as an exercise in the sheer joy of living.

But these high-tidal moments of life could not continue forever. They were brought to a sudden close on September 18, when Jefferson accidentally fell and broke his right wrist. Medical science in Paris was apparently a little crude; more than twenty visits to two doctors brought him little relief.

He received a note dated September 20 from Maria, who assured him that she felt "More uneasy, Than I can express." She had called at the legation the night before, but evidently he had retired and her visit had constituted only a "disturbance to your Neighbours." In her note she included an invitation to dinner: "I would serve you at dinner and divert your pain afterward with good music." [31]

Jefferson welcomed this pleasant diversion. But the Cos-

[31] Quoted in Jefferson, *Papers,* X, 393-394.

ways were planning to leave Paris, and Maria's tender
ministrations were soon to end. On the day of her departure Jefferson accompanied her to a brief luncheon at the
Pavillon de Saint-Denis. When this last repast was over,
he helped her to her carriage. Her husband was with her.
Jefferson said good-bye with misty eyes and drove back
alone to Paris.

That evening, "solitary and sad," he poured out his devotion in his unique "Dialogue of the Head and Heart":

Head: Well, friend, you seem to be in a pretty trim.

Heart: I am, indeed, the most wretched of all earthly beings.

Head: These are the eternal consequences of your warmth and
precipitation.

Heart: This is no moment to upbraid my foibles. I am rent into
fragments by the force of my grief.

Head: You will be pleased to remember I never ceased whis-
pering to you that we had no occasion for new acquaintances; that the greater their merits and talents, the more
dangerous their friendship to our tranquility, because the
regret at parting would be greater.

Heart: It was you, remember, and not I, who desired the meeting at Legrand and Molinos. I never trouble myself with
domes nor arches. But you, forsooth, who are eternally
getting us to sleep with your diagrams and crotchets, must
go and examine this wonderful piece of architecture. What
you had seen there was worth all you had yet seen in
Paris! I thought so, too. But I meant it of the lady . . . to
whom we had been presented. You, then, Sir, and not I,
have been the cause of the present distress.

Head: It would have been happy for you if my diagrams and
crochets had gotten you to sleep on that day. My visit to
Legrand and Molinos had a public utility for its object.
A market is to be built in Richmond. What a commodious
plan is that of Legrand and Molinos. While I was occu-

pied with these objects, you were dilating with your new acquaintances, and contriving how to prevent a separation from them. Every soul of you had an engagement for the day. Yet all these were to be sacrificed, that you might dine together. Lying messengers were to be dispatched into every quarter of the city with apologies for your breach of engagement. You particularly had the effrontery to send word to the Duchess Danville that, on the moment we were setting out to dine with her, dispatches came to hand which required immediate attention.

Heart: Oh! my dear friend, how you have revived me by recalling to my mind the transactions of that day! Go on then, like a kind comforter, and paint to me the day we went to St. Germain. How beautiful was every object! The wheels of time moved on with a rapidity of which those of our carriage gave but a faint idea. And yet in the evening when one took a retrospect of the day, what a mass of happiness had we travelled over!

Head: Thou art the most incorrigible of all the beings that ever sinned! I reminded you of the follies of the first day but instead of listening to these, you kindle at the recollection, you retrace the whole series with a fondness, which shows you want nothing but the opportunity to act it over again. You should abandon the idea of ever seeing them again.

Heart: May Heaven abandon me if I do!

Head: Everything in this world is a matter of calculation. Do not bite at the bait of pleasure till you know there is no hook beneath it. The most effectual means of being secure against pain is to retire within ourselves, and to suffice for our own happiness.

Heart: Yours is a wonderful proposition, to insulate ourselves, and to wrap ourselves in the mantle of self-sufficiency! Alone, the scene would have been dull and insipid. Let the gloomy Monk, sequestered from the world, seek unsocial pleasures in the bottom of his cell! Let the sublimated philosopher grasp visionary happiness, while pursuing phantoms dressed in the garb of truth! Their supreme wisdom is supreme folly. Had they ever felt the solid pleasure of one generous spasm of the heart, they would exchange for it all the frigid speculations of their lives.

Jefferson had recently felt many spasms of the heart when he looked at Maria Cosway, for all that he'd known her less than a month; and now he feared that he had written at inordinate length. As he wrote on October 12, he would even agree "to express but half my esteem for you for fear of cloying you with too full a dose. But, on your part, no curtailing. If your letters are as long as the bible, they will appear short to me. Only let them be brimfull of affection." [32]

Dr. Julian Boyd, the editor of the *Papers of Thomas Jefferson,* considers this letter to be "one of the most revealing in the entire body of TJ's correspondence, and one of the notable love letters in the English language." He believes that Maria had "momentarily captivated TJ," but was not sure of her victory when she received this letter. Dr. Boyd speaks with some certitude about Jefferson's control of his passions. He thinks that Maria had "but little understanding of the essential nature of the man to whom reason was not only enthroned as the chief disciplinarian of his life but also . . . was itself a sovereign to whom the Heart yielded a ready and full allegiance." [33]

It is apparent that Dr. Boyd knows little about Jefferson's emotional balance and less about the way of a maid with a man. If in Jefferson's case the head had really been sovereign, there might never have been the attempted intimacies with Betsy Walker. Jefferson's missive to Maria Cosway of October 12 is indeed "one of the notable love

[32] *Ibid.,* X, 443-453.
[33] Jefferson, *Papers,* X, 453-454, notes.

letters in the English language." It has all the earmarks of sincerity and could hardly have been part of a game of make-believe.

Before Jefferson had a chance to send this letter, he received a brief note from Maria, who had stopped at Antwerp. To this he replied on October 13:

> I found that your name was [appended] to four lines instead of four pages. I thank you for the four lines however because they prove you think of me. Little indeed, but better a little than none. I send you the song I promised. Bring me in return it's subject, *Jours heureux!* Learn it I pray you, and sing it with feeling.[34]

Jefferson signed his note, "Yours very affectionately."

Maria's October 30 response to Jefferson's letter of October 12 was coy. The "Dialogue of the Head and Heart" had been so well expressed it made her fearful that anything she might write would "appear trifling." Why did he say "so many kind things"? Why did he not leave her "a free consolation in admiring a friend? I honestly think my heart is invisable, and Mute, at this moment more than usual. It is full or ready to burst with all the variety of Sentiments which a very feeling one is Capable of." [35]

It is quite evident that Maria was deeply interested in Jefferson, but as her heart was "Mute," it was difficult for her to tell him in a graceful way just how strongly the tides of her "Sentiments" were running. She highly prized his letters and begged him on November 27 to write more frequently: "I have twice written without having a letter from you after the first which I found on my arrival here [London]. . . .

---

[34] *Ibid.*, X, 458-459.
[35] Quoted in *ibid.*, X, 494-495.

George Washington, engraving by A. H. Durand from the full-length portrait by Col. Trumbull belonging to Yale University. (All photographs relating to George Washington are used by courtesy of New York Public Library.)

Martha Dandridge Custis (Mrs. George Washington), engraving by J. Rogers from an original picture by John Woolaston. *(Lower left.)*

Sally Cary Fairfax, portrait from the book, *Sally Cary,* by one of the Cary descendants, George Miles Cary, privately published in 1916. *(Lower right.)*

Benjamin Franklin, a thumb portrait by Charles Willson Peale, after Martin. (All photographs relating to Benjamin Franklin, except for Madame Helvétius, are used by courtesy of The American Philosophical Society, Philadelphia.)

Deborah Read Rogers (Mrs. Benjamin Franklin), portrait attributed to Benjamin Wilson.

Wedgwood medallions of William Franklin (son) and William Temple Franklin (grandson).

Madame Helvétius, engraved on wood by Frank French, from a miniature in possession of M. Alfred Dutens. (Courtesy New York Public Library.)

Benjamin Franklin, portrait attributed to Van Loo, given to Madame Helvétius while Franklin was in France.

Martha Jefferson (daughter), miniature in possession of the American Embassy, Paris. (Courtesy Les Services Americaines d'Information.)

Martha Wales Skelton (Mrs. Thomas Jefferson), crayon portrait made for a friend by whose descendants in Mobile, Alabama, it is now owned. (Reproduced from *The Domestic Life of Thomas Jefferson* by Sarah N. Randolph.)

Thomas Jefferson, bust by Robert I. Aitken, in the Hall of Patriots, College of the City of New York.

Mrs. Maria Cosway, by herself, from a mezzotint by Valentine Green, in the collection of Mr. Edmund D. Martin. (Courtesy New York Public Library.)

Thomas Jefferson, portrait by Rembrandt Peale, 1805, when Jefferson was sixty-two and President of the United States. In possession of New York Historical Society. (Courtesy New York Public Library.)

Gouverneur Morris, portrait by James Sharples, 1810, now in possession of Mr. John Turnbull. Print from Frick Art Reference Library.

Talleyrand, portrait by Mlle. Godefroy. (Musée de Versailles, France.)

Adélaide de Flahaut, drawn by G. Staal, engraved by Massard, from a drawing by Chrétien. (Bibliothèque Nationale, Paris.)

Alexander Hamilton, engraving from a miniature by A Robertson. (Courtesy New York Public Library.)

Elizabeth Schuyler (Mrs. Alexander Hamilton), from an original picture painted in 1781 by R. Earl, now in possession of Mr. James Hamilton. (Courtesy New York Public Library.)

Every post-day I have waited anxiously. I take this occasion to send you a couple of lines . . . and to beg you to send me news of yourself." [36]

Jefferson had written to Maria on November 19, although, as he told her, "I write with pain" because of his broken wrist. She should know that if his hand "were able to follow the effusions of the heart, that would cease to write only when this shall cease to beat." [37] He told her on November 29 that his lonely heart forced his injured hand to move across the paper even though every word he wrote brought a spasm of pain. He cared not for this pain, however, and he would write more often if he were not certain that the letters he sent through the post office were read en route to her. Jefferson was a little fearful of the perils of the post office, and he preferred trusted couriers to take his letters to Maria. "The breathings of a pure affection would be profaned by the eye of a Commis of the poste. Could I write by the poste, I should trouble you too often; for I am never happier than when I commit myself into dialogue with you, tho' it be but in imagination." When this letter reaches its last paragraph, one can see very clearly that he was not just playing at love:

> I am determined when you come next not to admit the idea that we are ever to part again. But are you to come again? I dread the answer to this question, and that my poor heart has been duped by the fondness of it's wishes. . . . God bless you! May your heart glow with warm affection. Write to me often. Write affectionately, and freely, as I do to you. Say many kind things, and say them without reserve.[38]

[36] Quoted in *ibid.*, X, 552.
[37] *Ibid.*, X, 542-543.
[38] *Ibid.*, X, 555.

Apparently he also feared that frequent letters couched in warm, revealing phrases might prove too ardent for Maria. There were occasional lapses in his correspondence, and she would chide him sharply and enjoin him to write more often even if his notes were "blank sheets of paper."

But blank sheets of paper would not suffice for Jefferson. On Christmas Eve he wrote her a note that contained a gift of far greater value than precious jewels—a gift of fervent affection with all the words that lie between the lines lovers write when the heart laughs at caution. In his mind was always the question, when was she coming to Paris?

> You say not a word of coming to Paris. Yet you were to come in the spring, and here is winter. It is time therefore you should be making your arrangements unless you really mean to disappoint us. If you do, I am determined not to suppose I am never to see you again. I will believe you intend to go to America, to draw the Natural bridge, the Peaks of Otter &c, that   shall meet you there, and visit with you all those grand scenes. I had rather be deceived, than live without hope. It is so sweet! It makes us ride so smoothly over the roughness of life. . . . Think of me much, and warmly. Place me in your breast with those who love you most: and comfort me with your letters.[39]

But Jefferson's letters were delayed in delivery by the couriers to whom he entrusted them, and Maria's patience was sorely tried. She wrote on New Year's Day, 1787:

> I do not know for what offense I must suffer the anguish of Tantalus. Each day I expect that letter but the letter itself never comes. In your last letter—sent a century ago

[39] *Ibid.*, X, 627.

—you state that you had received one letter of mine; instead, I wrote no less than three. . . . You do not—what I have still more at heart—tell me how you are doing, and whether your arm is cured. These are topics sufficient to fill at least two lines; the consequence is not interesting, except to me, and you may write to give me pleasure. I will close with the assurance that I am always, with the same esteem and affection, your most affectionate and true friend.[40]

After Maria had received two letters from Jefferson, she took the time on February 15 to write him a long letter which covered many unrelated topics. She expressed her ardent desire to see the scenic wonders of rural America:

> Oh how I wish My self in those delightful places! Those enchanted Grotto's! Those Magnificent Mountains, rivers &c. Why am I not a man that I could set out immediately and satisfy My Curiosity, indulge My sight with wonders! I devote my evenings to Music and then I am Much visited by . . . Professors who come very often to play. Give me leave to remind you how Much pleasure you will give, to remember Sometimes with friendship One who will be sensible and gratefull of it as is yours, Maria.[41]

Maria's long absence from Paris cooled Jefferson's ardor a few degrees, and it was not until July 1, 1787, that he renewed his correspondence with her. A good part of his letter reads like a travelogue, and it is only toward the end that he asks once again the inevitable question:

> When are you coming here? If not at all, what did you ever come for? Only to make people miserable at losing you. Come then, my dear Madam, and we will breakfast

[40] Quoted in *ibid.*, XI, 3-4.
[41] Quoted in *ibid.*, XI, 148-150.

every day *à Angloise,* hie away to the Desert, dine under
the bowers of Marly, and forget that we are ever to part
again. I received, in the moment of my departure your
favor of Feb. 15 and long to receive another: but lengthy,
warm & flowing from the heart.[42]

In this letter to Maria, Jefferson did not express himself
with quite the intensity of some of his previous notes. The
very fact that he had neglected the correspondence for
six months was an indication that the head was once more
gaining a mastery over the heart. Maria realized this fact
and on July 9 she made a prompt reply:

Do you deserve a long letter, my dear friend? No, certainly not, and to avoid temptation, I take a small sheet
of paper; Conversing with you, would break Any resolution. . . . How long do you like to keep your friends in
anxiety? How many months was you without writing to
Me? . . . I do not know that we shall come to Paris this
year. I fear not. You cannot believe how much this uncer-
tainty displeases me, when I have everything to fear
against my desire. . . . It seems a dream to have been
there and I now wish it to be real, because of the impression it left upon me. . . . Tell me what comedies
there are that are new and everything that can induce
you to write me long letters.[43]

But Jefferson was now busy with family affairs and had
little time to write "long letters." In the summer of 1787
little Polly had come to Paris, and Jefferson tried to make
her acquainted with the sights. In the last week in August,
Maria made a sudden visit to Paris. This time her husband
did not accompany her. Once more Jefferson took her on

pleasure trips to Saint-Germain-en-Laye and Versailles, but the glow of the previous year was absent. He paid more attention to official correspondence, and on weekends his two daughters took up much of his time. Maria could see the difference in his attitude toward her and tried to hide her dismay by immersing herself in the gay social whirl of Paris. She neglected to write to London, and John Trumbull wrote to Jefferson on September 17 that Maria's friends, including her lonesome husband, were "not only angry at her for not writing, but suffer all the distress of anxiety least illness or accident of any kind should have occasioned her silence." He commissioned Jefferson "to scold her heartily." [44]

In reply, Jefferson wrote Trumbull on October 4 that he could not carry out his commission until he "could get a machine for scolding invented, because it is a business not fit for any human heart, and especially when to be directed on such subjects as her." [45]

But at times Jefferson felt the need of a scolding machine, because Maria had so many social engagements that she had little time for him. He complained of her parsimony in doling out hours during which they could get together. Before Maria left to return to London, Jefferson gave a "great dinner" in her honor during her last week in Paris, and she remarked in a December 1 note that she deeply regretted having seen him infrequently during the four months she had been in Paris:

If my inclination had been your law, I should have had the pleasure of seeing you More than I have. I have felt the *loss* with displeasure, but on My return to England

[44] Quoted in *ibid.*, XII, 138-139.
[45] *Ibid.*, XII, 143.

when I calculate the time I have been in Paris, I shall not
believe it possible. At least if that could soften my regret,
I shall encourage My imagination to favor Me.[46]

On the evening of December 7, Jefferson received a note
from Maria telling him that she could not have breakfast
with him on the following morning: "To bid you adieu
once is sufficiently painful, for I leave you with very melancholy ideas." [47]

Maria left Paris before dawn on December 8 and thus
missed a farewell scene with Jefferson. On December 10,
with revealing promptitude, she wrote Jefferson from
London and confessed for a second time that the reason
she had seen him rather seldom in Paris was that he had
not pressed her to give him more time. If he had acted
with more decision, he could have fixed the times for their
meetings.

I left Paris with Much regret indeed. I could not bear to
leave any More. I was Confus'd and distracted. You Must
have thought me so when you saw me in the Evening.
Why is it My fortune to find Amiable people where I go,
and why am I to be obliged to part with them! T'is very
Cruel: I hope our Correspondance will be More frequent
and punctual than our Meetings were while I was in
Paris. I suspected the reason, and would not reproach you
since I know your Objection to Company. You are happy
you can follow so Much your inclinations. . . . Accept
this short letter this time. I Mean to send a Much longer
One soon, but Mean while answer me this by a long one.[48]

Jefferson answered Maria's letter on the last day of January, 1788, telling her he had gone to her residence to have

[46] Quoted in *ibid.*, XII, 387.
[47] Quoted in *ibid.*, XII, 403.
[48] Quoted in *ibid.*, XII, 415.

breakfast with her but that she had already left for London. This fact spared him

> . . . the pain of parting, but it deprives me of the comfort of recollecting that pain. . . . In your case it was not my fault, unless it be a fault to love my friends so dearly as to wish to enjoy their company in the only way it yields enjoiment, that it, en petite comité. You make everybody love you. You are sought and surrounded therefore by all. Your domestic cortege was so numerous, et si imposante, that one could not approach you quite at their ease.[49]

Jefferson was now finding excuses for not having seen more of Maria while she had been in Paris. If he had really wanted to re-establish their relationship on the 1786 basis, he could have insisted that she give up her constant round of pleasures and put aside some time just for him. She was evidently hoping that he would do just that, but for him the former thrill was over and there was no use rekindling an old flame that had burned out.

Maria sensed this situation and wrote to Jefferson on March 6 to reproach him for his failure to write her as regularly as he had formerly done. She was not willing to accept the fact that his ardor had dwindled so:

> I have waited some time to trie, if I could recover my usual peace with you, but I find it is impossible yet, therefore Must address Myself to you still *angry*. Your long silence is unpardonable, but what is the Name I must give to ——— Mr. Trumbull and Mrs. Church [for] not bringing Me a letter from you? No, My war against you is of such a Nature that I cannot even find terms to express it. Yet I will not be in your debt. I think it is a great One since it is to acknowledge *one* letter from you, *One* and

[49] *Ibid.*, XII, 539-540.

short, however I believe that really you know how I value
every line which comes from you, why will you add scar-
city. But I begin to runn on and my intention was only
to say *nothing,* send a blank paper; as a Lady in a Passion
is not fit for Any thing. What shall you do when you will
be Much farther, I can't bare the idea?[50]

In London, Maria was constantly asking John Trumbull
for news about Jefferson. Although she professed to be
angry with him for his neglect in writing to her, she repeatedly asked John Trumbull to convey her affectionate
regards to Jefferson, and she also asked Trumbull to procure for her a small portrait of Jefferson.[51]

In the first three weeks in April, 1788, Jefferson took an
extended trip through Germany, and when he returned to
Paris on April 23 he found a letter from a "lady in a Passion." The next day he hurriedly wrote her a long answer.
During his trip he had often thought of writing to her, but
"sometimes the fatigue of exercise, and sometimes fatigued
attention hindered me." After writing an interesting travelogue on Germany, he struck a personal note in his last
paragraph:

I came here [Paris] and received your angry letter. It
is a proof of your esteem, but I love better to have soft
testimonials of it. You must therefore now write me a letter teeming with affection such as I feel for you. So much
I have no right to ask. Being but just arrived I am not *au
fait* of the small news affecting your acquaintances here.
. . . When you come again therefore you will be somewhat nearer to me, but not near enough: and still surrounded by a numerous cortege, so that I shall see you

50 Quoted in *ibid.,* XII, 645.
51 Quoted in *ibid.,* XII, 647.

only by scraps as I did when you were here last. The time before we were half days & whole days together & I found this too little. Affectionately.[52]

A greatly mollified Maria answered this letter from London on April 29. She feared she could not visit Paris in the near future. Why could he not visit London?

We should go to see Many beautiful villas, enjoy all the best England can afford & make the rest up with our own society; we shall not have a Numerous Cortege, I promise to Make Myself & my Society according to your wish. If I come to Paris I may do more what I please this time, there are but four people I could wish to pass all my time with, is this too great a Number? when *you* are One, even if you dont guess the others I am Sure you would not object to.[53]

Under the impact of these affectionate sentiments, Jefferson's mercurial affection took a move upward. Behind his gay banter flowed an undercurrent of warmth. On July 27 he responded to her notes of April 29 and July 15. He was glad that she was not enmeshed in the bright social web of earlier months and was becoming something of a recluse: "A great deal of love given to a few, is better than a little to many." This letter ends with a warm plea: "Adieu, my dear friend, love me much, and love me always." [54]

Three days later, disturbed over her letter of July 15 with its chiding tone, he sent her a hasty note asking her not to be too impatient:

52 *Ibid.*, XIII, 103-104.
53 Quoted in *ibid.*, XIII, 114-116.
54 *Ibid.*, XIII, 423-424.

I am incapable of forgetting or neglecting you, my dear
friend; and I am sure if the comparison could be fairly
made of how much I think of you, and you of me, the
former scale would greatly preponderate. Chide me then
no more; be to me what you have been; and give me without measure the comfort of your friendship.[55]

Jefferson's letters to Maria Cosway show him to have
been something of a weathervane. At times there was an
indication of cool breezes and medium temperature, but
this could quickly change to warm currents of air with a
rapidly rising temperature. The head obviously did not
always control the heart.

On August 19 Maria wrote that she had been "Made
very uneasy with the news that you intend to return soon
to America. Oh then I give up the hopes of ever seeing
you again." [56] Five weeks later, on September 26, Jefferson
confirmed the news that he would return to America, but
he would not be gone from Paris for long: "Maybe as short
as five months." [57] On December 23 Maria sent Jefferson a
note introducing a Mrs. Hannah Cowley: "Take care of
your heart, she may run away with it." At the end of the
note she made the plea, "Pray write, pray write, pray write,
& dont go to America without coming to England." [58]

As the New Year opened Jefferson began to feel the
approaching French Revolution. After a short review of
the news of mutual friends in Paris, he remarked in the
last paragraph of a January 14 letter to Maria Cosway:

[55] *Ibid.,* XIII, 435.
[56] Quoted in *ibid.,* XIII, 524-525.
[57] *Ibid.,* XIII, 638-639.
[58] Quoted in *ibid.,* XIV, 372.

We are so apt to believe what we wish that I almost believe I shall meet you in America, and that we shall make together the tour of the curiosities of that country. Be this as it may, let us be together in spirit. Preserve for me always a little corner in your affection in exchange for the spacious part you occupy in mine.[59]

The letters that still passed between Maria and Jefferson had now reached the safe plane of sincere friendship, although it is difficult to imagine how Jefferson, even in fancy, could conceive that he and Maria could go sightseeing together in America. But it was a pleasant mental tidbit to play with, and on February 6, 1789, Maria remarked: "You are going to America and you think I am going with you. I thank you for the flattering compliment. I deserve it for I shall certainly be with you in spirit. I shall walk thro' the beautiful scenes you will describe to me by letter." [60]

On his journey back to America in October, 1789, Jefferson's ship was detained for a few days in Cowes, England. On the fourteenth, he decided to brighten the dull hours of leisure by writing to Maria a letter in which he continued on a high plane the game of hearts: "Once and again, then, farewell. Remember me and love me." [61]

After Jefferson returned to America, his arduous duties as secretary of state in Washington's cabinet interfered with his correspondence with Maria. When he retired from these official activities in 1794, he was still extremely busy as the leader of the slowly emerging Republican Party, the forerunner of today's Democratic Party. The

[59] *Ibid.*, XIV, 445-446.
[60] Quoted in *ibid.*, XIV, 525-526.
[61] *Ibid.*, XV, 521.

pace of his correspondence with Maria slackened considerably, and when he did write the tone of unabashed affection was no longer present. When he was inaugurated as President in 1801 she wrote him a letter of congratulation that ended upon a note of nostalgia:

> Could you permit a thought that time or distance has at all rescind[ed] my interest in what attends you. I shall flatter myself with the certainty of your remembrance toward me. Send me a few words to assure me I live in your esteem & friendship & you will revive the happiness of yours affectionately, Maria.[62]

Jefferson replied that she could be assured of his "deepest and sincere affection and respect." The pressure of presidential business was too unrelenting to afford him much time for correspondence with her. She could not understand this official urgency, and she kept writing him letters complaining that he was neglecting her: "Surely you have not forgotten such an old friend!" [63] But with Jefferson the high fires of his years in Paris had died down to a steady glow of mature friendship. The French Revolution had made a profound change in the France he had known so well and loved so deeply, and he indulged in no more dialogues of the head and heart.

As the years passed, his correspondence with Maria lost the color and informality of youth. Unlike Washington's final letter to Sally Fairfax, Jefferson did not send to Maria a passionate missive in which his long pent-up feelings burst through the stout walls of the decorum that usually hedges in American Presidents.

[62] Quoted in Bullock, *op. cit.*, pp. 152-153, 160-161.
[63] Quoted in *ibid.*, p. 160.

Jefferson left the White House in 1809, and in the liberal atmosphere of Monticello he had many opportunities to open his heart to Maria; but the old urge was gone forever, and his retrospections now took him neither to Paris nor to London. He went back to the years of his youth when he had gaily courted Martha Skelton at the Forest and brought her home to Monticello where, for a decade, all their dreams had come true.

In 1821, Maria wrote to him of the death of her husband and once more alluded to a trip to Monticello: "I would pay you a visit if it was ever so much out of my way, but it is impossible. The remembrance of a person I so highly esteem and venerate, affords me the happiest consolation." Two years later she expressed a desire to watch the development of the University of Virginia: "I wish I could come and learn from you." [64]

She was never able to visit Monticello and see the magnificent vista that was so dear to Jefferson's heart. But the project of a university sponsored by Jefferson inspired her to found a school for girls at Lodi, Italy.

The correspondence closed when Maria was sixty-five and Jefferson eighty-one. Her final letter is filled with quiet contentment. Her days in Paris with Jefferson were still a fragrant memory, and she hoped he would tell her more about Monticello and the recently established University of Virginia. But death tapped Jefferson on the shoulder before he could answer her inquiries, and she lost all interest in Monticello. Twelve years later she died at her school at Lodi. I have often wondered whether she ever showed her pupils the "Dialogue of the Head and Heart."

[64] Quoted in *ibid.*, pp. 185-190.

four

Gouverneur Morris
[1752-1816]

YOUTHFUL PURSUITS

In recent years there have been many monographs by learned pedagogues in the field of sociology who boldly assert that children born of parents who are in comfortable financial circumstances tend to have larger intellectual endowments than children born of parents who inhabit skid row. The parents of Gouverneur Morris were never confronted with the danger of falling into anything like John Bunyan's slough of despond financially. Indeed, if one can borrow a phrase from (among others) Edgar Allan Poe, who lived for a brief period in a New York slum, it is apparent that Gouverneur was born "to the purple." His father was a highly respected landed proprietor, whose ample fortune ensured that his last son by a second marriage would move in the best circles of an affluent New York society. There is no doubt that Gouverneur inherited a superior intellectual endowment which deeply impressed his contemporaries, and it led him to the comfortable belief that his own abilities "were more adapted to the deliberations of the Cabinet than the glorious [military] labors of the field." [1]

His mother, Sarah Gouverneur, came of introspective Huguenot stock and was thus not inclined to waste much affection upon a brood of children. Young Morris was never close to his mother, but in later years he was indeed avid for feminine affection, and it is possible that his rapid pace along the primrose trail was in search of the warm affection his mother never showered upon him. He remains an interesting challenge to some biographer familiar with the techniques developed by Sigmund Freud and applied in fascinating detail by Stefan Zweig in his absorbing study of Marie Antoinette.

In the will of Gouverneur's father there was an instruction that he should receive "the best possible education provided that it not be at Yale." This meant that he would probably be sent to King's College, later Columbia University. In preparation for a college education he was sent to a Huguenot academy in New Rochelle, where he acquired a limited fluency in the French language. In later years, when he became the American minister to France, this language training was of great assistance to him in official conversations and in the preparation of state papers. In

[1] Gouverneur Morris, *A Diary of the French Revolution,* ed. B. C. Davenport (Boston, 1939, 2 vols.), I, VII.

Paris he soon discovered that he needed an expert assistant in formulating replies to searching questions from the
French foreign minister. He usually relied upon a "sleeping dictionary" with a beautiful cover and definitions that
always satisfied him. But she could not accompany him to
the Foreign Office and participate in diplomatic conversations. He was a bold man, however, and he carried on
these conversations with a great deal of spirit, which reminds one of Talleyrand's comment upon the conversational ability of the Duke of Wellington: "He speaks French
with great intrepidity."

In both written and spoken English, Gouverneur had a
fluency that attracted wide attention. This talent was
already evident in his address at the commencement at
Columbia University when he received his master of arts
degree. The topic was, "Love, the Bright and Steady Lode-
star of the Moral World." Gouverneur thought he knew a
great deal about love, and developed that theme at considerable length; there were certain young ladies of his
acquaintance who thought that his facility in that regard
was entirely too expert.

KITTY LIVINGSTON

One of Gouverneur's close friends was William Livingston,
who made up for the misfortune of having been educated
at Yale by bringing into the world two lovely daughters,
Kitty and Sally. At eighteen Gouverneur was already
aware of Kitty's charms, and on a rare May morning in
1770 he tried to storm her heart by a barrage of words that
had at least the merit of rhyme:

Know then, dearest Kitty, thy note I received
And that sooner you came not would sorely have grieved,
Had Lewis not told me that your short Delay
By continuing longer you richly would pay.
To welcome you hither each tree shall appear
In the gayest apparel he wears thro the year,
And the fragrance of May shall invite you to rove
And join with the songsters which people each grove.
For thee every beauty more fair shall be seen,
More blooming the Blossoms, more virdant the green.

A year later, after he had been admitted to the bar, he tore himself away from the dry *Commentaries* of Blackstone and became a votary of Venus. Once more it was Kitty Livingston to whom he addressed a verse, this one dated November, 1771:

Love, thou tender Foe to Rest,
Soft Disturber of the Mind
Ease at length my Troubled Breast
Sweet Tormenter now be kind.[2]

Morris's poems, like those of George Washington, did not open the heart of the girl he wished would show him some marks of affection. Perhaps he would do better in prose. On May 2, 1772, he sent Kitty a letter in which he pleaded for letters that would indicate her interest in him. He also made a request that every lover has made of the mistress of his heart since the game of love was invented— he would like a lock of her hair.

[2] These verses, and the correspondence quoted on the next several pages, are found in the archives of the Massachusetts Historical Society, Boston.

According to my Promise I send you some Pens and I send them upon a Condition that you also will perform a Promise made which they will in some sort enable you to do. You know you are much my Debtor on the Letter Score; at Least I know you have Confessed so much and I am firmly resolv'd to be paid, if it be by mere plaguing of you untill you do it. . . . I much fear that you will not take Pleasure in making a Return . . . untill some Leisure Moment offers itself in which you will have Nothing to do but think of an Absent Friend. The more frequently they occur the greater will be my Happiness I assure you. They will relieve my Mind when it is too much disposed to wish and wish the Hours away, a sensation which, dear Kitty, you are by no means unacquainted with and consequently know how painful it is. . . . Pardon me for renewing to you my frequent Request that you would favour me with a small Lock of your Hair which indeed I shall wear devoutly as a Sacred Relick.

In her return letter, dated July 10, Kitty confessed that she did think of him occasionally, but she reproved him for an insinuation he had made in his last letter. He replied at once that he was glad that she sometimes thought of him:

You cannot guess how happy I am from the Consideration that at Length for one Moment I have been the Subject of your Meditations. I most heartily wish I would invent or discover some method by which those Moments might be made more frequent. . . .

I am, believe me, very sorry to have insinuated any thing to any Person which you do not like. I would never have done it wittingly or willingly. . . . I am a very bad hand at Explanations and will attempt one upon this express

Condition only, that it will be agreeable to you. Where
that is the Case I would do any Thing.

You threaten me much but I fear you are only a Bully.
. . . I am fully determined when I call upon you in the
Jerseys, to put some crow quills in my Pocket. I hope I
may not forget it.

The temperature of the affection Morris entertained for
Kitty was rising every day, and on August 16, 1772, he
avowed his love for her:

Every day and every hour I feel a more violent inclination to enjoy your company and conversation and I realize
very clearly that without them I am happy by halves only,
yet I take no pains whatever to quell these emotions tho'
it is a thousand to one that I shall find them extremely
troublesome for you acknowledged that once you warmly
loved (Susan says five times). It is therefore clear that
I am a fool and you are a judge how unmistakable a hopeless Passion of this kind is.

When Kitty wrote to Morris on August 29 and excused
her lack of more frequent correspondence by referring to
a painful injury to her ankle, Gouverneur was most for-
giving. Few people write with their ankles, but he did not
allude to that fact:

Had you written me that you had a pain in your ankle
I should on that principle have been satisfied. My Time
is very pleasantly spent in the dreaming Way. I generally
converse with you by that Means at least once every three
days or rather Nights and you will grant that I must be
very happy during that Time. I tell you what, Kitty, I do
not like your Letter and I will tell you why. You tell me
a great big Lie in it; and you do it knowingly and willingly

which is worse and you do it to catch a Compliment which
is worse still, and you do it to one who knows all this,
which is worst of all—you hussy. Do you think that the
more I know you the less I like you? Not you. Ain't you
ashamed then to say so—fie, fie, fie. And after this when
the Consequence stares you full in the face, you bring
yourself with another abominable Lie, that you are imprudent and then with most matchless effronterie call
upon one to vouch for the Truth of such an Assertion. But
see you, impudent baggage, what will happen and see the
Judgment that awaits you. Henceforth learn not to bear
false Witness against yourself and your Neighbour. Know
then that I do not merely assert the clear contrary and
moreover I do aver that in my Opinion you are as Amiable
as *I* would wish any Woman and as prudent as you need
be.

This note with its gay banter reminds one of Shake-
speare's *Taming of the Shrew,* and it is likely that Gouverneur had that comedy in mind when he sent his sophisticated letter to Kate. But the effort spent on this letter must
have exhausted him, for there is a long gap in his correspondence with Kitty. Finally he sent her a letter on
August 30, 1773, and explained that a press of business
affairs had been taking most of his time. He wished, however, to know in "minute detail" just what she had been
doing. He ended on a characteristically flippant note that
the young lady did not receive well: "What will come will
be right whether or not agreeable to me."

This affectation of philosophic pragmatism combined
with a swaggering devil-may-care attitude did not please
Kitty, and it certainly displeased many of Gouverneur's
friends. Apparently he heartily agreed with Voltaire, who
once gaily remarked, "I look upon solemnity as a disease."

But Voltaire had written many serious books that served as an acceptable ballast to his levity. Morris was as yet only half-baked, and he had a long way to go before people would concede that he had outstanding mental gifts that compensated for his irrepressible tendency to be flippant when he should be serious.

FROM LANGUID LOVER TO ACTIVE PATRIOT

In Massachusetts after 1770 the Sons of Liberty, aided by unwitting merchants, began to light fires of discontent with imperial rule that soon grew into a major blaze of revolution. Sparks from these fires began to ignite tinder in New York City, and on May 19, 1774, the ever-active Sons of Liberty called a public meeting to discuss the situation. From a safe coign of vantage, Morris noted the movements of the excited populace, and on the following day he wrote to John Penn in Philadelphia and described his reaction to the first signs of revolution in New York. He made it clear that he felt no sympathy for the radicals, and he expressed the opinion that it was to the "interest of all men to seek for reunion with the parent state." He was contemptuous of the "riotous mob": "Poor reptiles! it is with them a vernal morning; they are struggling to cast off their winter's slough, . . . and ere noon they will bite." [3]

In another letter he mentioned a plan for "uniting the whole continent in one grand legislature," but he regarded such a scheme as "hopeless." [4] Boston patriots were more

[3] Quoted in Jared Sparks, *Life of Gouverneur Morris with Selections from His Correspondence and Miscellaneous Papers* (Boston, 1832, 3 vols.), I, 23-26.

[4] Quoted in *ibid.*, I, 26-27; see also Daniel Walther, *Gouverneur Morris, Witness of Two Revolutions* (New York, 1934), pp. 17-18.

farsighted, and on June 17 a call went out for a general congress to meet in Philadelphia on September 5. This first Continental Congress continued in session until October 26, with no talk of independence. In the meantime, the Convention of New York succeeded to the functions of the old colonial Assembly, and in June, 1775, it selected Morris and three of his associates to form a committee to wait upon General Washington while he was passing through the city. Washington was en route to Boston where he was to assume command of the Continental armed forces.

Washington suffered a disastrous defeat at the Battle of Long Island. Morris stayed with the army during the retreat across the Jerseys, and from Boonton he wrote to the New York Convention to explain his absence. It was in his usual flippant tone, and it furnished fresh ammunition to his enemies, who were often more articulate than his friends.

But as a member of the Continental Congress, Morris rendered General Washington invaluable service. He consistently supported Washington as myopic opponents tried to belittle his abilities and push him aside in favor of intriguing incompetents who had more brass than brains. At times, however, Washington found it necessary frankly to inform Morris that his ideas on the conduct of hostilities, especially with reference to levying large contributions upon the city of Philadelphia, would "inflame the country and lay the foundation for much evil."

Even during the trials of war Morris never lost his sharp wit, and his gay verbal sallies made some of his contemporaries regard him as a trifler with no real ability. This fact is well illustrated in the following comment of John Adams in 1779 to the French Minister to America, the Chevalier de la Luzerne:

Gouverneur [Morris] was a man of wit and made pretty verses; but of a character *très léger*. That the cause of America had not been sustained by such characters as that of Gouverneur Morris or his colleague, Mr. Jay, who was also a young man about 30 and not quite as solid as his predecessor Mr. Laurens.[5]

John Adams's opinion that Morris was best known as a man of wit and a dabbler in verse was fairly close to the mark. Even Gouverneur's intimate friend John Jay made sly allusions to his lovemaking proclivities. In a letter to Robert R. Livingston he made a direct reference to one of Morris's characteristic "foibles": "Gouverneur is daily employed in making Oblations to Venus." [6]

Jay was named by the Continental Congress as the American minister to Spain, and Morris visited Philadelphia in October, 1779, to say farewell to his friend and his beautiful wife, Sally. Morris knew, of course, that his old flame Kitty Livingston would be there to bid her sister good-bye. Kitty had been spending the summer months in the Quaker city, and her father had written to warn her not to be an "immodest nor an unpatriotic flirt." This admonition did not apply to Morris, and it was not needed.

[5] John Adams, *Works,* ed. C. F. Adams (Boston, 1850-1856, 10 vols.), III, 219.

[6] Quoted in Frank Monaghan, *John Jay, Defender of Liberty* (Indianapolis, 1935), p. 276.

MORRIS LOSES A LEG IN PURSUIT
OF FAIR WOMEN

Kitty Livingston regarded Morris as an incorrigible flirt. She had taken his measure in the years of her youth, and he no longer fitted into her thoughts for the future. This was unfortunate for him, because if his "Oblations to Venus" had been made before her shrine he would have been saved from an accident that seriously affected his life.

From the usual accounts of this accident, it would appear that on May 12, 1780, Morris was thrown from a phaeton he was driving at high speed, and that his left leg was caught in a wheel and so badly mangled that an amputation was imperative. According to wicked gossip, the cause of this misfortune was that Morris had been engaged in making "Oblations to Venus" before a very attractive lady when an irate husband interrupted the ritual and Morris took to hasty flight. Morris was so intent upon escaping, so the tale went, that he pushed his horses at a reckless speed that made the accident inevitable.

From John Jay we get an insight into the story behind the accident. In a letter to Morris of mock consolation, he remarked, "I have learned that a certain married woman after much use of your Legs has occasioned your losing one." [7] And in writing to Robert Morris (who was no relation to Gouverneur, incidentally), Jay made a statement that students of Freud could interpret in many ways: "Gouverneur's Leg has been a Tax on my Heart. I am almost tempted to wish he had lost something else." [8] Lord

[7] Quoted in *ibid.*, p. 219.
[8] Quoted in *ibid.*, p. 219.

Palmerston, father of Queen Victoria's prime minister during the American Civil War, met Gouverneur in Paris and was favorably impressed. In his diary he made the following statement concerning Morris: "He has only one leg, having been obliged to undergo an amputation in consequence of jumping from a window in an affair of gallantry." [9]

After his accident Morris was taken to the home of Colonel George Plater, where, as Jared Sparks observes, "He received every attention, which kindness and sympathy could dictate." [10] Recovery from the amputation was long and painful. Morris was finally fitted with a plain wooden leg which he wore with an air of bravado. During the months of his slow recovery he was unduly appreciative of the tender ministrations of the beautiful Mrs. Plater whose many kindnesses he never forgot. A decade later, when he was a resident in London, there is an entry in his diary for May 5, 1790, which engages a reader's attention:

Just as I am coming away from this place (the home of Mrs. Joanna L. Beckford), Mrs. Beckford informs me that Mrs. Plater is dead. I get away as soon as possible that I may not discover Emotions which I cannot conceal. Poor

[9] Quoted in *ibid.*, p. 219; "Diary of the Second Viscount Palmerston France, July 6-August 21, 1791," *The Despatches of Earl Gower* (Cambridge, 1885), pp. 283-310.

[10] Sparks, *op. cit.*, I, 223. In an editorial note, B. C. Davenport, in Morris, *op. cit.*, I, 504, makes the following comment upon Mrs. Plater: "Elizabeth Rousby, married to George Plater in 1764. When Morris lost his leg, Philadelphia, 1780, he was nursed in the house of this Maryland Member of the Continental Congress. Several years Eliza's junior, his gratitude had its romantic side."

Eliza! My lovely friend; thou art then at Peace and I shall behold thee no more. Never, Never, Never.[11]

Morris seldom grew so emotional in his diary, and it indicates the depth of his attachment to Elizabeth Plater. But at least he did not kiss and tell. An entry in the diary some weeks later gives another indication that Gouverneur had not been the only man who had read the writing on the walls of her heart, and he knew instinctively that beauty such as hers had evoked from many warm hearts the same songs of love that the skylark pours forth each morning to greet the miracle of dawn. In his diary he tells a little gossip about Eliza:

I go at three to take up Mrs. Low but she is not yet dressed. . . . She has been twice to Ranelagh and has the Appearance of much fatigue for which I scold a little in Jest and have some reason to believe that my Conversation is not disagreeable. In the evening she tells me many Things respecting Mrs. Plater which I am surprized at her Knowledge of.[12]

FINANCES AND THE NEW AMERICAN NATION

As the military phases of the American Revolution were coming to an end, it was apparent to American statesmen that some radical action would have to be taken with

[11] *Ibid.,* I, 533.

[12] With reference to Mrs. Low, B. C. Davenport observes: "Gentle, handsome Mrs. Low, daughter of Colonial Mayor Cuyler, of Albany, and wife of Isaac Low of New York. . . . When Victorious New York State proscribed him, confiscating his property, departing Loyalist was the only role left him" (in *ibid.,* I, 190).

regard to American finances. The Articles of Confederation went into operation in March, 1781, but the new federal government was sorely handicapped by the fact that it had no source of assured income. Congress now turned to Robert Morris and made him superintendent of finance, with Gouverneur Morris as his able assistant. Robert Morris soon saw the hopeless nature of the task of bringing order into a financial system that had no adequate taxing power, however, so he and Gouverneur resigned their federal offices and went into a series of ambitious financial ventures of their own.

Gouverneur, realizing that Robert was somewhat reckless in his business dealings, arranged to have much of his own capital and many of his business deals handled through William Constable and Company in New York. He showed unusual business ability and soon built up a large fortune which he was able to maintain to the end of his days.

The budding American nation had dire need of a constitution that would bind the thirteen states into a firm union with adequate powers for effective government. The federal Constitutional Convention was called for this purpose, and it met in Philadelphia from May 25 to September 17, 1787. Gouverneur Morris was one of its most active delegates. James Madison, the real father of the Constitution, wrote to Jared Sparks in 1831 and paid a high tribute to Morris' work at the Convention: "The finish given to the style and arrangement of the Constitution fairly belongs to the pen of Mr. Morris; the task having, probably, been handed over to him by the chairman of the Committee. . . . A better choice could not have been made."[13]

[13] Quoted in Sparks, *op. cit.*, I, 284-286; see also Howard Swiggett, *The Extraordinary Mr. Morris* (Garden City, 1952), pp. 115-132.

After his labors at the federal Convention were over, Morris prepared to take an extended sojourn in England and France, primarily for business reasons. He was particularly interested in business opportunities arising out of speculation on the payment of the large American debt to France. He surely believed, too, that in Paris pleasure would go hand in hand with all kinds of business opportunities, and his wooden leg was a constant reminder that he could use a lot of warm, feminine affection to pay the price of that lost limb.

MORRIS LEARNS THE FRENCH LANGUAGE

Morris landed at Le Havre after a tempest-tossed voyage of forty days. He was glad to push on to Paris, and his life there is told in great detail in a diary so colorful that its unexpurgated edition was not published until 1939. It begins on March 1, 1789, and is the best source of information on Morris's long stay abroad.

After establishing a residence in the Hotel de Richelieu and presenting his many letters of introduction, he was ready to begin his unofficial mission in France. He soon discovered that his knowledge of the French language was imperfect, and in the different salons he visited he realized that much of the wit and badinage passed over his head: "Not being perfectly Master of the Language, most of the Jests escape me." [14] It was evident to him that he badly needed the right kind of dictionary: a female one. He was not long in finding her.

On March 5 he called on Jefferson, then minister to France, and was taken to the Foreign Office and intro-

[14] Morris, *op. cit.*, I, 4.

duced to the Comte de Montmorin. He also met the Comte d'Angivillier, a brother of the Comte de Flahaut, and was fortunate enough to become acquainted with Madame de la Fayette, Madame Duplessis, and the Duchesse d'Orléans, whose beauty was striking and whose fidelity to a wastrel husband was the talk of Paris. On March 9 he supped with the Comte de Puisignieu and got an insight into the temper of the ladies of Paris: "The Women, I observe, all pay a very kind Attention to the Baron de Bezenval, whose grey Hairs designate rather the Father than the Lover. But it seems he has been remarkably successful in seducing the Sex. At present he receives a Kind of Worship for his former good Deeds." [15]

On March 21 Morris had his first look at the lady who would serve not only as his dictionary but also as a charmer who would soon introduce him to what Paris called the "Cyprian mysteries." She was Adélaide de Flahaut, who at eighteen had married the Comte de Flahaut, fifty-three. This gap of more than three decades had been bridged by a corrupt priest, Charles Maurice de Talleyrand-Périgord, Bishop of Autun. Napoleon once termed Talleyrand a "silk stocking stuffed with filth," and this description was quite apt. That acidulous characterization brings to mind Victor Hugo's mordant description of the famous French critic Sainte-Beuve as "exquisite and vile."

Sainte-Beuve had entered Hugo's hearth like a serpent and had stolen from him his much-beloved wife, Adèle. Talleyrand had played to perfection a similar role with the Comte de Flahaut, whose wife was also called Adèle. But his remarkable command of language had enabled him to mollify the outraged husband to the extent of accepting the results of the seduction. Their son, Auguste-

[15] *Ibid.,* I, 9.

Charles-Joseph de Flahaut de la Billarderie, grew up to be the dashing Comte de Flauhaut, aide-de-camp to Napoleon and later Ambassador to England.

At dinner with Madame Cabarrus, Morris met Adèle de Flahaut. He noted in his diary that she was "a pleasing Woman, not a sworn Enemy to Intrigue." [16] Morris was attracted at once by Adèle's warm, bright beauty. According to the portrait painter Vigée-Le Brun, Adèle had "the wittiest eyes in the world." Some said that her large brown eyes had the quality of velvet. The fact that she had an illegitimate son by Talleyrand, Bishop of Autun, did not deter Morris from promptly setting out to pursue her. On the contrary, her interesting past spurred him to hope that history might repeat itself. This repetition was not long in occurring.

Adèle could be of service to Morris in many ways. Her little salon in the Louvre was a meeting place for some of the most distinguished men in Paris. These contacts were invaluable to him, and under her tender tutelage his knowledge of the French scene was greatly widened and his vocabulary enlarged to include words dealing with dalliance in affairs of the heart. She had a mental agility that amazed him, and in later years Paris was not greatly surprised when she produced a series of novels that were widely read and favorably received. Indeed, Sainte-Beuve praised them as "the perfume of the eighteenth century." The most remarkable feature of her creative activity was the fact that she wrote *Adèle de Sénanges* in her salon during innumerable interruptions. Her love affair with Morris helped give authentic detail to her story.

On March 31, 1789, Morris paid a call at Adèle's apartment. In his diary that evening he wrote a few revealing

[16] *Ibid.*, I, 17.

comments about her: "An elegant Woman and a snug
Party. She is by no Means deficient in Understanding and
has I think good Dispositions. *Nous verrons.*" [17] He called
at the Louvre several more times to see Madame de Flahaut and confirm his impression of her elegance, but she
was not at home, so he forgot affection for a brief time and
on April 29 wrote a letter to President Washington on the
state of morals in France. It was not a pretty picture that
he drew:

> The Materials for a Revolution in this Country are very
> indifferent. Every Body agrees that there is an utter Pros-
> tration of Morals, but this general Position can never con-
> vey to an American Mind the degree of Depravity. . . .
> An hundred Anecdotes and an hundred thousand Exam-
> ples are required to show the extreme Rottenness of every
> Member. . . . Inconstancy is so mingled in the Blood,
> Marrow and very Essence of this People that when a Man
> of High Rank and Importance laughs today at what he
> seriously asserted Yesterday, it is considered as in the
> Natural Order of Things. . . . The great Mass of the
> common People have no Religion but their Priests, no
> Law but their Superiors, no Morals but their Interest.[18]

Morris was not too concerned about the morals of the
French women, and he had no scruples about talking with
certain beauties while they took their leisurely baths in
their salons. In order not to shock his American modesty
too greatly they usually mixed milk with the bath water,
thus making it difficult for his eyes to define their arresting
curves. On June 21 he went again to the Louvre to call
upon the attractive Madame de Flahaut:

[17] *Ibid.,* I, 25.
[18] *Ibid.,* I, 61.

She seems inclined to make me her Confidant: but for what? She talks to me of certain Affairs of Gallantry which she has been told I was once engaged in. I assure her that these are idle Tales. I assure Her of a Truth that I never lost my Respect for those who consented to make me happy on the Principles of Affection.[19]

While Morris was laying siege to Adèle's heart, the situation in Paris was growing more tense every day. He was visiting the residence of an important business associate, Laurent le Couteulx, on July 14 when the news came of the storming of the Bastille: "The Governor . . . is beheaded, and the Prevost des Marchands is killed and also beheaded; they are carrying the Heads in Triumph thro the City." [20]

During those days of bloodshed and violence, Morris continued his search for the key to Adèle's heart. Finally, on July 20, he asked for a showdown:

Make a long visit; at first tête à tête. Give her some Verses and with infinite Coolness and Seriousness tell her that I cannot consent to be only a Friend, that I know myself too well. That at present I am perfectly my own Master with Respect to Her, but that it would not long be the Case. That having no Idea of inspiring her with a Passion, I have no Idea either of subjecting myself to one. That besides, I am timid to a Fault. That I know it to be wrong but cannot help it. She thinks it a very strange Conversation, and indeed so it is, but I am much mistaken if it does not make an Impression much greater on Reflection than at the first Moment.[21]

[19] *Ibid.*, I, 119.
[20] *Ibid.*, I, 148.
[21] *Ibid.*, I, 157.

While going to call on Adèle the following evening, Morris saw a sight that chilled his blood. A wild mob had murdered Monsieur de Foulon, who had just accepted a place in the ministry: "The Head on a Pike, the Body dragged naked on the Earth. Gracious God! what a people!"

On the morning of July 23 Morris got a note from Adèle requesting him to come to her apartment. It was evident that the tide of her love was slowly moving toward him:

> After Dinner we slide insensibly into the same Conversation we had last Monday. It has I find made the Impression I expected. However, to cure me of the Passion, she avows a Marriage of the Heart. I guess the Person. She acknowledges it and assures me that she cannot commit an Infidelity to him. By Degrees however we come very near it. A sudden Thought prevents for this Time. Question: whether our Connection is to break off or go farther.[22]

Morris was hopeful that his "Connection" with Adèle would indeed "go farther." He went to see her at the Louvre on July 26, and promised her he would consult with the Committee on the Constitution at Versailles the following day as to the content and style of this instrument of government. Adèle was very appreciative of his cooperation in this matter, and his conquest of her heart made definite progress: "We have a little wild Chit Chat. She takes Precautions against any Scene like that of Friday. But we convince each other of our very warm Esteem and that Opportunity might perhaps ripen this Esteem into active Affection."

The following day he called on her again and had a

[22] *Ibid.*, I, 160.

new experience. He watched her going through her toilet arrangements in the presence of her husband, who did not seem to mind having Morris as an interested spectator:

> She is at her Toilet. Monsr. comes in. She dresses before us with perfect Decency even to the Shift. Monsieur leaves us to make a long Visit and we are to occupy ourselves with making a Translation. We sit down with the best Disposition imaginable but instead of a Translation. . . .[23]

On July 30 Morris left for London, where he had many business appointments. Robert Morris's financial affairs were becoming more tangled every day, and Gouverneur realized that it would be difficult to satisfy the importunate creditors. Gouverneur was interested in at least meeting beautiful women in London, and so asked Jefferson for a letter of introduction to Maria Cosway. Somewhat regretfully Jefferson complied, but in the letter to Maria he inserted a precautionary phrase:

> Receive into your peace and grace the bearer hereof Mr. Morris, a countryman & friend of mine, of great consideration in his own country, & who deserves to be so everywhere. Peculiarly gifted with fancy & judgment, he will be qualified to taste the beauties of your canvas. The Marquis Luzerne, an old and intimate acquaintance of his, will bear witness to you of his merit. But do not let him nestle me out of my place; for I still pretend to have one in your affection, tho' it is a long time since you told me so.[24]

[23] *Ibid.*, I, 164.
[24] Quoted in Helen D. Bullock, *My Head and My Heart* (New York, 1945), p. 116.

Maria's response must have disturbed Jefferson a bit.
The return letter to the American legation in Paris was
delivered to Jefferson by Maria's brother George, who had
long been eager to meet the American minister at Paris.
The note read: "I am quite in love with Mr. Morris. Are all
Americans so enjoying as those I know? Pray take me to
that Country, your description has long Made me wish to
see it, & the people I know confirm my desire." [25]

Jefferson did not need to worry that Morris might "nes-
tle" him out of Maria's heart. Gouverneur had really taken
scant notice of the London beauties, and was longing to
be back in Paris. As soon as he returned to his Paris apartment he hurriedly called upon Adèle:

> She says we must be chaste, which I agree to. After
> Dinner we chat and laugh but approach to a breach of
> her Orders, when she receives a Note from the Bishop of
> Autun. He is to be with her at Half Past Five. She insists
> that I leave her at five. I put on a decent Share of Cold-
> ness and oblige her to solicit Embraces which I refuse.
> This disconcerts her very much; however, at last I confer
> the Joy repeatedly and promise to return to Supper. [26]

Morris had at last made his conquest of Adèle's heart,
although that "mitred Monster," Talleyrand, was still in
the running. At times he insisted upon calling at the Louvre
even when Morris was there, and had the added temerity
to stay so late that Morris went home to the arms of Mor-
pheus while the Bishop enjoyed Adèle's. It is certain that
Talleyrand never bothered to return to the arms of Mother
Church.

But Adèle insisted upon having time for enjoying pleasures with Morris. She had apparently forgotten about her decision to be chaste, as we see from this entry in Morris's diary:

> Go to the Louvre. Madame is still suffering. She has followed my prescription but hitherto unsuccessfully. After being with her a few minutes I exhibit another Medicine which works Wonders. The Roses blush on her Cheek, her Eyes sparkle; she assures me repeatedly that she is very well. We go to her Convent and visit her Religieuse. We return and celebrate the Cyprian Mystery. I then leave her to receive the Bishop.[27]

Morris was proud of his prowess in this "mystery," and he recorded in his diary that he believed he could "wean her from all Regard" for the Bishop, whose heated embraces were too importunate for Adèle. The secret was that he "wants the *fortiter in Re*" but still had the power to proceed with "*suaviter in Modo*."

The Bishop had no intention of permitting Morris to be Adèle's only patron. At times he claimed that he went to the Louvre only to see his child, little Auguste-Charles-Joseph. Morris called at the studio after one such visit by the Bishop:

> She dwells much upon her Child and weeps plenteously. I wipe away the tears as they fall. This silent Attention mingles by Degrees the sexual with the maternal Affection. . . . According to custom on such Occasions the genial Bliss opens a female heart to lavish Professions of endless Love. She means every Word of it now, but nothing here below can last forever.[30]

[27] *Ibid.*, I, 281.
[30] *Ibid.*, I, 275.

It was apparent to Morris that the Bishop was a formidable rival who would continue to visit Adèle upon one excuse or another. Morris decided to accept the situation as it existed and make no protests. On October 29 he took Adèle and little Auguste-Charles-Joseph for a walk through the Tuileries. When they returned to the Louvre, the Bishop promptly made his appearance and Morris left Adèle to "a Tête à Tête with him." But he later returned because "Madame is waiting for me. We celebrate the Cyprian Mystery to her great Satisfaction." The next day he stole a march upon the impassioned Bishop and visited the Louvre early, where he performed "the usual Rites, which are not the less acceptable for being repeated." [31]

Elated with this success over the Bishop, on the following day Morris paid such an early visit to Adèle that he caught her in her bath. She invited him to talk with her during this immersion, and casually informed him that it was usual to receive visits in the bath: ". . . and I suppose it is. . . . After she comes out of the Bath and gets into Bed I exhibit a cordial and restorative Medicine which has been in great Repute ever since the Days of Adam, and then leave her to Meditation and repose." [32]

Fortunately for Morris, the Bishop became increasingly involved in the political vortex that was engulfing Paris, and therefore was a less frequent visitor to the Louvre. The entire burden of responding to Adèle's passion was joyfully assumed by Gouverneur: "After Dinner we pass two hours together in perfect Delight. My amiable friend is wound up to a Delirium of Enjoyment." [33]

[31] *Ibid.*, I, 276-277.
[32] *Ibid.*, I, 300-301.
[33] *Ibid.*, I, 315.

MORRIS VISITS ENGLAND

On October 13, 1789, President Washington sent Morris instructions to guide him during informal talks with the British foreign secretary on the best way to smooth the growing asperities in Anglo-American relations. Morris left Paris during the last week in March, 1790, and had an audience with the Duke of Leeds on the twenty-ninth. President Washington had been particularly anxious to know what the British government intended to do with regard to the western posts which they had continued to hold after 1783 in contravention of the peace treaty. The President also wanted to know when the Foreign Office would send the United States a minister and thereby accord recognition to the newly organized government under the Constitution.

On March 29 Morris went to Whitehall and handed the Duke of Leeds a personal letter from President Washington. When the Duke expressed himself with some "warmth of Approbation" concerning the friendly tenor of Washington's message, which gave assurances of a desire to cultivate amicable relations between England and America, Morris made a tart reply: "I am very happy, my Lord, to find that such Sentiments prevail, for we are too near Neighbours not to be either very good Friends or very dangerous Enemies." The Duke was slightly embarrassed by the tactics of Morris, who then proceeded to ask some questions that did not admit of glib answers.[34]

After this verbal bout with the Duke of Leeds, Morris went to dinner at the home of his half-brother Staats Lane

[34] See *ibid.,* I, 464-466.

Morris, who had risen to the rank of lieutenant general in the British army. Immediately after this solemn repast Morris went to "Mrs. Low's Rout," which was more colorful:

> Mrs. Kennedy, in good spirits, invites my Attentions. I, of course, bestow some small Share. Mrs. Mallet seems not unwilling to extend her Dominion but this will not do for me. Converse with Mrs. Phyn. Beauty, Sense and Softness joined, but I have vowed Fidelity upon another Altar.[35]

In moving around in London society Morris met Charles James Fox, sporting British statesman, and James Boswell, biographer of Dr. Samuel Johnson. Gouverneur also dined with Maria Cosway and took her to the Drury Lane Theatre, but the beauty and piquant charm that had conquered Jefferson were lost on Morris, who could not keep his mind off the seductive attractions of Adèle, back in Paris.

On May 21 Morris had another session with the Duke of Leeds at Whitehall. William Pitt, the prime minister, attended this session, and Morris tried to touch his pride about the British government's holding the western posts for more than a decade in contravention of the Treaty of Paris. Pitt refused to be stampeded into any concessions to America, and the Morris mission ended in complete failure.[36] In matters of the heart the mission might also be called a failure, because Morris had developed no real desire to pursue any of the beauties of London.

In the last week of September, 1790, he prepared to leave London, and as a farewell gesture he and Boswell

[35] *Ibid.*, I, 477.
[36] See *ibid.*, I, 597-600.

decided to attend the theater. As his journal amply discloses, Boswell was inordinately fond of "wenching," and after the show he was eager to demonstrate to Morris his lusty disposition. But feminine temptation in a gross form sickened the American, who complained to his diary about the spectacle: "The Herd of Prostitutes at this Theatre and the open, shameless Conduct of those who handle and converse with them, is in my opinion a Reflection upon the Taste if not the Manners of this Country. [Came] Home in Spite of their kind Invitations." [37]

MORRIS BECOMES MINISTER TO FRANCE

Morris left London in the last week in September and made a leisurely return journey to Paris. On October 6 he was back home but his many months in England had made some difference in his relations with Adèle. She was not so demonstrative in her welcome as he had expected, and he remembered the old saying, "Out of sight is out of mind." He was also disturbed by the fact that she had a new admirer, young Lord Wycombe, who seemed very much at ease at the Louvre. Adèle, of course, assured Morris of her fidelity to him and tried to convince him that during his absence she had been "cool" and very "wise." He felt "obliged to doubt both a little."

He soon discovered that her old admirer, the Bishop, was still in attendance at the Louvre, and frequently practiced "*fortiter in Re*" with "*suaviter in Modo*":

I walk to the Louvre. Monsr. is with her. . . . After some Time Monsr. is called and as I consider this to be a Rendezvous understood, I am for proceeding imme-

[37] *Ibid.*, I, 601.

diately to the Object, but I find that she has formed Her plan too and it is now a Question to be meerly her friend. I tell her that this cannot be but if she wishes to get Rid of me Nothing is so easy, and immediately wish her a Good Morning. Of Course I am entreated back and Monsieur presently after comes in. He stays some Time and when he is gone we have a strange mingled Scene of Sentiments, Caresses and some Tears, which last do not come easily. At length she tells me that Matters are accomodated between her and the Bishop and so well accomodated that nothing but the entry of Monsr. de Flahaut a few Days ago prevented him from doing the Needful. Having told me this, she says I may if I please possess her. I agree to do so *pour la dernière fois*. She says I am a Cheat in telling her it is for the last Time.[38]

Adèle was right in calling Morris a cheat: in subsequent weeks history often repeated itself. But Morris did not possess her for himself alone. Lord Wycombe insisted on sharing some of the pleasures, and the omnipresent Bishop occasionally claimed her under the right of prior possession. On the morning of February 24, 1791, Morris went to the Louvre and found Adèle in tears. She confided to him that she had returned home the previous evening to discover that the Bishop had been to her apartment and had left in a blank envelope a copy of a will he had executed making her his beneficiary. In her last conversation with him he had threatened suicide. She hoped he had not carried out this threat because he was scheduled that very day "to consecrate two bishops lately elected." What sort of perverted episcopacy he would consecrate them to she did not mention.

Morris soon discovered that the Bishop was very much

[38] *Ibid.*, II, 55.

alive. He was evidently too cowardly and too selfish to commit suicide, and when he finally made his appearance at the Louvre he demanded that Adèle return the will he had made for her benefit.

But the Bishop's noisome presence at the Louvre and the thought of his prowess in the sexual as well as the diabolical arts reduced the temperature of the affection Morris entertained for Adèle several degrees. Maybe he had better look elsewhere. On May 9 he called to see how the hunting would go at the home of Madame de Nadaillac:

> She has a Gentleman with her. . . . We get rid of our Companion with Difficulty and then from one Thing to another we come very near to the Consummation but she is refractory and talks much Religion and Morality. I leave her angry a little, but more I think because I did not persevere than because I went as far as I did.[39]

But Morris soon found that further adventures with Madame de Nadaillac were impossible. His position in Paris was about to undergo an important change, and official business would soon take most of his time. On January 12, 1792, Morris' nomination to be minister to France was confirmed by the Senate. Jefferson's letter announcing his formal appointment was written on January 23, but he did not receive this official dispatch until April 6.[40] The first word he got concerning the appointment came in a letter from his old friend Robert Morris.

Before this news arrived, Morris had been considering the purchase of the famous Macomb tract of land in north-

[39] *Ibid.*, II, 180.
[40] See *ibid.*, II, 396-406.

ern New York. Adèle then renewed to him "her assurances that she will go with me to America." [41] But this American idyl was abandoned when he received official news of his appointment as American minister to France.

Jefferson included in his official dispatch a word of caution about any expression of opinion with reference to the many different governments that might be established in Paris, and Morris assured Jefferson that he would be most careful in that regard. On January 28 President Washington frankly informed Morris by letter that some senators had opposed his appointment and had charged him "with levity and imprudence of conversation and conduct," and that it was thus "indispensably necessary that more circumspection should be observed by our Representatives abroad." [42]

On June 3 Morris was presented to the King and Queen, and his mission formally began. He realized that France was on the eve of revolution. In a dispatch to Jefferson shortly after his reception by the King, he remarked: "We stand on a vast Volcano, we feel it tremble and we hear it roar but how and when and where it will burst and who may be destroy'd by its Eruption it is beyond the Ken of mortal Foresight to discover." [43]

Lafayette was pitifully weak in the face of popular demonstrations and the National Guard was loath to follow his leadership. Fundamental political changes were just a few weeks away. Morris viewed the rapid erosion of royal power with dismay, and he saw with deep concern the tides of revolution finally sweep away all the familiar landmarks in Paris. The city he loved so ardently became

[41] See *ibid.*, II, 346.
[42] Quoted in *ibid.*, II, 402.
[43] *Ibid.*, II, 449.

a place of terror, and he feared for the lives of those who were close to him.

In view of this situation he paid little attention to President Washington's admonition to preserve "circumspection" with regard to the rapidly changing governments of France. Instead he took an active part in political affairs, and prepared a plan for the escape of the King and Queen from Paris. Large sums of money from the royal treasury were brought to the American legation for safety, and Morris was involved in many schemes to safeguard important court members. In this regard Adèle played a significant role, and her translations of Morris' official notes were invaluable. A typical entry in his diary is that of July 27, 1792:

> This morning Brémond calls and afterwards Monciel. We work all the Morning to prepare some Memoirs for the King. I have a large Company to dine with me and after Dinner I take my friend [Adèle] to her Convent where we embrace *en attendant la Religieuse.* Afterwards go to the Louvre and spend the Evening there.[44]

But time was running out for Morris and Adèle. On August 5 he went to the court: "Nothing remarkable, only that they were up all Night expecting to be murdered." It was not long before these fears were realized. Stark tragedy was moving in Paris with such swift feet that love affairs were pushed aside, and Morris' and Adèle's romance was nearing its end. On the evening of August 9, 1792, Morris went to the Louvre and possessed Adèle for the last time. They had been lovers for more than three years, though their warm embraces had often been inter-

44 *Ibid.,* II, 481.

rupted by the unannounced entry of Adèle's husband or
by the stealthy slide of the Bishop's club foot over the
thick salon carpet.

On August 10 the mob murdered the Swiss Guard, and
the National Assembly suspended the authority of the
King and Queen. Adèle, in terror, sought sanctuary in the
American legation, and Morris was able to provide a
means of escape for her and her little son. When he next
heard from her she was in London but hoped she would
soon be able to return to Paris. But on January 4, 1793,
she sent him a note which put a period to their tempestu-
ous love affair:

> Not a line from you and yet I write, and will even
> always write. . . . I have done all I should and even
> more than I should; I don't know whether you owe me
> any gratitude, but I don't feel guilty in the least for hav-
> ing abandoned you for so long. I claim the right of sacri-
> ficing you as much as myself when serious misfortunes
> call me. I complain to you, and with you, but it seems to
> me there can be no question of excuses between us be-
> cause, on my side at least, there can be no wrong. . . .
> Good-bye, my dear and good friend; I am in the best of
> spirits at the thought of seeing you soon.[45]

This note shows little of the ardor that Adèle must once
have felt for Morris, but one has to remember that at this
time she was writing her novel Adèle de Sénanges, and
her affair with Morris was supplying graphic detail for her
fiction. At any rate, she was safe in London for the time
being, and her modest "lodging" on Half Moon Street
was conveniently paid for by her new lover, Lord Wy-

[45] *Ibid.*, II, 600-601.

combe. By some strange quirk of fate, the now unfrocked Bishop was in London too, and he limped to her lodging with the same regularity that had marked his importunate calls at the Louvre. Fortunately for Adèle, the sensual charms of a Madame Grand had become increasingly attractive to the Bishop, who furthermore would soon leave for a thirty-month sojourn in America.

As for Morris, his conduct as Minister to France had not been pleasing to President Washington, who sent James Monroe to Paris in the summer of 1794, as the new minister. In commenting upon his own mission Morris remarked: "I will neither praise nor excuse it but confine myself to the sincere wish that my successor will act with more wisdom in a situation less critical." [46]

Morris forgot his failure as minister by indulging in another love affair, this time with Madame Simon. But when he left Paris she had no desire to accompany him on his travels and frankly informed him of that fact. Despite her lack of warmth he still entertained some affection for her, and after their parting he confided to his diary: "We parted with strong emotion which affects me much." [47] There was nothing to do now but move on to Switzerland.

In Altona, near Hamburg, he rented a house for Adèle. But she had no desire to begin another chapter in her life with a cast-off lover like Morris. She was a unique person who had faced misfortune with rare courage and was ready for new adventures. She had not permitted even serious financial difficulties to stop her progress on her novel *Adèle de Sénanges,* which, when published in London, evoked widespread favorable comment which in

[46] *Ibid.,* II, 401.
[47] *Ibid.,* II, 586.

turn meant satisfying sales. As a well-known novelist she began to attract new admirers, and in 1802 she married José Maria de Souza Botelho, the Portuguese ambassador to France. Her salon became once more the gayest in Paris.

LOVE AT THE FAMILY FIRESIDE

Morris finally returned to Morrisania on January 5, 1799, after an absence of a decade. He had a passionate attachment to country life. His first months in Morrisania were spent in carrying out a program of extensive improvements upon the manor house, which he had found "leaky and ruinous," and in intensive cultivation of fields that had long been fallow. His election to the United States Senate interfered with some of his domestic arrangements, but it put him in the public eye at a most important time in American history. The presidential election of 1800 had resulted in a tie vote between Jefferson and Burr, and when Jefferson entered the White House after a close contest, it seemed like a page from yesteryear for Morris to visit his old friend and discuss world affairs.

But Morris needed a feminine hand to direct the servants at Morrisania and to give him some measure of the affection he so desperately yearned for. In Paris he had found in Adèle a warm woman who had laughed at all the values men usually place upon the women they love, and yet her wanton actions had merely deepened the desire he had felt grow stronger each day. And this desire was a mixture of many things. It was not merely born of her beauty and her wealth of physical attraction; it had had an intellectual side that intrigued him. Adèle had displayed conversational talents that surprised him, and in her salon she had held her own with some of the most subtle minds in Paris. She had polished the state papers that Morris submitted to the French Foreign Office, and helped give distinction to his style both in speaking and writing. Her many novels published after Morris left Paris were eloquent testimonials of her talent as a writer and her evident ability to plumb the depths of human nature. She was passion and elegance in a mold that had few equals.

Morris was well aware of Adèle's unique qualities, and he never sought to find her equal on the American scene. He wanted warmth and understanding, and he finally found them in a woman who was looked at askance by his friends and with revulsion by her own family.

In 1789 Morris had made a brief trip to Virginia and had stayed a few days at Tuckahoe, the plantation of Colonel Thomas Mann Randolph. There he saw as a young girl Nancy Randolph, and doubtless was attracted by her youthful beauty. But Nancy soon fell upon evil days. She was seduced by her brother-in-law, Richard Randolph, and it was widely rumored that she had murdered a child born to her in September, 1792. Nancy and Richard Randolph had been indicted for murder in April, 1793, and it had taken all the eloquence of Patrick Henry to save them from punishment.

Nancy had no personal fortune, and so it was necessary for her to live with her Randolph relatives until it became impossible for her to stand the hostile atmosphere that surrounded her. The fact that she did not collapse under this strain proved that she had a core of unshakable character that could not be broken by bitter circumstance. It is difficult to pick up the threads of her life after she fled the Randolph plantations and sought work with acquaintances in the North. Her situation was well described in a grim descriptive phrase that Francis Thompson once applied to the trials of the Irish poet James Clarence Mangan —he was a man who had "a charred past and a bleared future."

Morris introduced the bright gift of sunshine into Nancy's life. In October 1808, he called at her boarding house in Greenwich Village, New York City, and announced to her that he hoped "some reduced gentlewoman would undertake to keep his house, as the lower class of house-keepers of his provoked the servants to a riot in his dwelling." [48]

While Nancy was considering this offer of employment, he wrote her a letter in which he consolingly remarked: "I once heard but have no distinct recollection of events which brought distress into your family. Dwell not in them now. If we ever happen to be alone you shall tell your tale of sorrow when the tear from your cheek may fall into my bosom." This expression of sincere sympathy touched her deeply, and the last paragraph of his next letter persuaded her to accept his invitation to take charge of the house-keeping arrangements at Morrisania: "I cannot close this letter without telling you again that my esteem and affection are undiminished, perhaps encreased. God be with you and comfort you and make you happy and blessed." [49]

As Nancy read between the lines of this message she knew that happiness awaited her in Morrisania. She answered his letter affirmatively, and Morris welcomed her

---

[48] Nancy Randolph Morris to Joseph C. Cabell, May 30, 1828; quoted in William C. Bruce, *John Randolph of Roanoke, 1773-1833* (New York, 1922, 2 vols.), II, 300.

[49] The letters of Gouverneur Morris to Nancy Randolph are in his *Letter Book,* preserved in the Library of Congress with his manuscript papers.

to Morrisania with a cordiality that wiped away all questions. His long attendance at the court of love had made him unusually perceptive about affairs of the heart, and during the long December evenings at Morrisania he and Nancy arrived at an understanding that was deep and lasting and unashamedly warm. He loved the Greek and Roman classics and he had always admired the poet Horace, who had achieved to perfection that much-loved combination of tenderness and disillusion. In Morris this warm admiration of Horace led to close imitation, and Nancy, at last, found the affection she had not dared dream of.

On Christmas Day, 1809, Morris and Nancy had many of his friends and relatives to a gay dinner. At its conclusion he suddenly announced that he and Nancy planned to be married at once. The solemn rites were performed that day in Morrisania, much to the consternation of relatives who had hoped to inherit all of his ample fortune. In his account of this ceremony, Jared Sparks has the following brief paragraph: "On the twenty-fifth of December, 1809, Mr. Morris was married to Miss Anne Cary Randolph, a lady accomplished in mind and person, and belonging to one of the ancient and most respectable families in Virginia." [50]

There is no whisper of wicked gossip in this brief account of the marriage, and sleeping dogs were allowed to lie in quiet contentment until they were kicked into a noisy chorus by the Randolph family, which seemed to resent Nancy's good fortune. In December, 1811, Morris and Nancy paid a visit to Washington, and John Randolph of Roanoke came to see Nancy at Tomlinson's boarding house. According to Randolph, Morris had requested that he visit Nancy, and he finally consented. He remarked that the main reason he had decided to call on Nancy was

[50] Sparks, *op. cit.*, I, 494.

to ascertain whether "any change of circumstances" had made any "change" in her conduct. He had hoped that she had seen "the errors" of her ways.[51]

Nancy's meeting with the malignant John Randolph brought on a spell of illness that made it impossible for her to travel for several days. But Morris stayed in good health and moved on to Albany, where he was occupied in pushing through the legislature a bill providing for the construction of an Erie canal. When he returned home on June 23, he made the following illuminating entry in his *Diary:* "Dear, quiet, happy home." It was on this night that Nancy told him that she was pregnant. Thus she was tied to him with the strongest bond that Mother Nature could devise. But the atmosphere of this "quiet, happy home" was soon polluted with poison gases that followed a visit by the Randolphs to Morrisania.

In July, 1814, Tudor Randolph, son of Nancy's sister Judith, wrote to Nancy and requested money to pay his expenses to Morrisania, where he hoped he might be nursed back to health. Nancy sent the money and Tudor arrived at Morrisania on August 4 with a Harvard College classmate as an additional burden. When Judith heard of her son's serious illness she hastened to Morrisania and received an affectionate welcome from Nancy, whose life she had done so much to make unbearable. On October 22 John Randolph arrived as a guest at Morrisania, and embraced Nancy and kissed her on the lips. It was not long before he acted in the tradition of the Duke of Alva, whose dagger had always "followed hard upon his smile." That night Tudor, who had been tenderly nursed by Nancy, whispered to John Randolph that Nancy was clandestinely indulging in "lewd amours." This accusation was

[51] Quoted in Bruce, *op. cit.,* II, 274-278.

believed by the foul mind of Randolph, who vented his filth upon Nancy when he left the following day. In a letter addressed to Nancy dated October 31, 1814, he remarked as follows:

> When, at my departure from Morrisania, in your sister's presence, I bade you remember the past, I was not surprised of the whole extent of your guilty machinations. I had nevertheless seen or heard enough in the course of my short visit to satisfy me that your own dear experience had availed nothing toward the amendment of your life. . . . Unhappy woman, why will you tempt the forbearance of that Maker who has, perhaps, permitted you to run your course of sin and vice that you might feel it to be a life of wretchedness, alarm and suspicion? You now live in the daily and nightly dread of discovery.[52]

This letter is clear evidence of the disordered mind of Randolph, who was bent upon poisoning Morris' feelings for Nancy. To carry out this dark design he wrote a long letter to Nancy which he cunningly addressed to Morris. On receiving it, Morris kept it for a while without speaking to Nancy about it. All the filth that had long lain dormant in Randolph's mind now poured forth in a malodorous stream of calumny that makes it one of the most malignant letters in American history. And this was not all. Randolph was intent upon spreading the vile charges against Nancy as far and wide as possible. Relatives and friends of Morris were told of Nancy's alleged wicked past, and Randolph hoped that her ruin was securely and permanently established.

But fortunately for Nancy, Morris immediately rejected Randolph's charges and strongly asserted his belief in her

[52] Quoted in *ibid.*, II, 274 ff.

innocence. In a letter to Randolph Harrison, Morris gave his view of the whole affair: "Mr. Randolph's communication gave me no concern, for Mrs. Morris had apprised me of the only fact in his possession, before she came to my house, so that her candor had blunted the point of his arrow." And then, as a sharp shaft at the Randolph clan for leveling false and vile charges against one of their own members, he spoke of how his heart had been deeply touched for "the houseless child of want that I took to my bosom." [53]

This wretched conspiracy of the Randolphs to complete the ruin of a girl they had done so much to destroy collapsed entirely in the face of the utter disbelief Morris showed with reference to their baseless charges. He would have preferred to drop the whole matter, but Nancy insisted upon writing a reply to John Randolph, on January 16, 1815. It was as sharp and as true as a Toledo blade:

My husband yesterday communicated to me for the first time your letter of the last of October, together with that which accompanied it. . . . It seems, Sir, as if you wished to apprize Mr. Morris and him only of circumstances important to his happiness and honor, though fatal to my reputation, leaving it in his power to cover them in oblivion or display them to the world as the means of freeing him from a monster unfit to live. But this was mere seeming. Your real object was widely different. Under the pretext of consulting Com. Decatur and Mr. Bleecker, you communicated your slanders to them, and then to Mr. Ogden. . . . You have professed a sense of gratitude for obligations you suppose my husband to have laid you under. Was the attempt to blacken my character and destroy his peace of mind a fair return? . . . When you entered this

[53] *Ibid.*, II, 277.

house, and when you left it, you took me in your arms,
you pressed me to your bosom, you impressed upon my
lips a kiss which I received as a token of friendship from
a near relation. Did you then believe that you held in your
arms, that you kissed the lips of a common prostitute, the
murderess of her own child and of your brother? Go, tell
this to the world that scorn may be at no loss for an object.[54]

Nancy was fluent in her denunciation of all the base
charges that had been broadcast against her character,
and yet she realized that despite her fluency there would
be some credulous persons who would believe the worst
against her. But she could hug to her heart the knowledge
that the person whose opinion counted most was the very
person who would hotly reject them—her husband. Morris knew that the world had been good to him. He had
searched the world over for the affection he most wanted,
like the quest for the bluebird of happiness, and he had
found it at his family fireside. In a letter to John Parrish of
July 6, 1816, he gave an intimate picture of the love and
happiness that pervaded the atmosphere at Morrisania:

I lead a quiet, and more than most of my fellow mortals,
a happy life. The woman, to whom I am married, has
much genius, has been well educated, and possesses, with
an affectionate temper, industry and a love of order. Our
little boy grows finely, and is generally admired. You may,
then, opening your mind's eye, behold your friend, as he
descends with tottering steps the bottom of life's hill, supported by a kind companion, a tender female friend, and
cheered by a little prattler, who bids fair, if God shall

[54] Quoted in Bruce, *op. cit.*, II, 278-295.

spare his life, to fill in due time the space his father leaves.[55]

I do not think that any husband in the evening of his life could write a more pleasant word picture of life around a family fireside with love fanning the embers into a warm, comforting glow. Nancy could have looked back upon the tragic years when in Virginia she had cowered in the shadows of the Randolph firesides and have whispered in the spirit of a later Andrew Lang poem, "Dark and true and tender is the North."

[55] Quoted in Sparks, *op. cit.*, I, 495.

five

Alexander Hamilton
[1755-1804]

THE MAN AND THE MYTH

Many years ago Woodrow Wilson, in speaking of Alexander Hamilton, made a revealing observation: "A very great man, but not a great American." In this terse description he gave the essence of Hamilton's personality. Of Caribbean birth, he possessed the early maturity that occasionally marks the inhabitants of that area, and he soon gave evidence of the genius that seems often to accompany a blending of Scottish and French racial stocks. He was a transplant who shone to great advantage in his American environment. It was fortunate that he arrived on this continent at a moment that was propitious for his ample talents to reveal themselves. Great national crises do not create great men; they merely unveil them. When Hamilton arrived in Boston the great events of the American Revolution were just a few years off, and the stage was set for a drama in which he would speak some inspired lines and receive the warm acclaim of an American audience that was beginning to experience the first birth pangs of nationhood.

During his youth on the Danish island of St. Croix he came under the influence of a Presbyterian divine, Hugh Knox, who not only molded his mind against the oppressive imperial taxation but who was a prime mover in Hamilton's emigration to continental America. Hamilton's rapid development in the friendly atmosphere of New Jersey and New York is a familiar story to most Americans. His unusual ability as a pamphleteer who favored colonial claims was proved by his lengthy publications, which were marked by cogent reasoning and polemical skill of a high order. It is remarkable that colonial audiences took the time and had the inclination to peruse pamphlets that ran to inordinate length, and it is apparent that Hamilton was impressive at least by the weight of his utterances.

At an early period Hamilton rejected the proverb that the pen is mightier than the sword, and we find in his letters the oft-expressed hope that he would be able to achieve an important military reputation. In the Continental Army he soon attracted Washington's friendly interest and was an important officer on his staff. The fluency and clarity of his style made him an ideal secretary, and Washington was delighted that his rough drafts of correspondence could be quickly translated into letters and orders that were models of terse and effective expression.

But Hamilton soon tired of his post as secretary to the commander in chief, and yearned for an assignment that would bring him military renown. One day when his patience had worn thin and Washington's demands were a little importunate, his temper flared into easy rebellion and he turned in his resignation. His letter to his father-in-law, General Philip Schuyler, describing his break with Washington reveals an unlovely side of Hamilton's personality. He was unduly sensitive to fancied slights, and his critical comments about Washington indicate a surprising ingratitude for the many kindnesses, and blindness to the noble qualities of his military superior. These qualities of Washington's were soon called into evidence when Hamilton boldly asked him for a command at the siege of Yorktown where he might win a modest military reputation. Brushing aside any feeling of annoyance at Hamilton's impertinent actions connected with his abrupt resignation from his staff, Washington gave him the assignment he requested and thus permitted him to win the military honor he was so anxious to achieve.

But Hamilton's thoughts were not always on military affairs. During the middle of the war he wooed and won the hand of Elizabeth Schuyler, fair daughter of General Schuyler, who owned many broad acres and whose wealth lent an aureate splendor to Betsey's ready smile. The story of this fortunate marriage is one of the bright romances among our founding fathers, and the shadows that darkened this love idyl merely confirmed the fact that Hamilton's blood had a tropic accent that stressed beauty in the feminine form even when it was not within the family circle. That chapter in Hamilton's life will be told later.

CARIBBEAN BACKGROUND

There are many questions about Alexander Hamilton's exact date and place of birth. It has generally been assumed that he was born in Charlestown, island of Nevis, on January 11, 1757, but the birthplace is still somewhat in doubt and the date was probably 1755, not 1757. The biographies of Hamilton by his son and grandson are filled with inaccuracies. The first biographer who went to the British and Danish West Indies and searched through musty records on him was the novelist Gertrude Atherton, who tells of her researches in her usual fascinating manner. After looking through the archives in the islands of St. Kitts and St. Croix, she went to Copenhagen and found some startling data there. In her *Adventures of a Novelist* she makes certain interesting statements concerning one Rachel Lavien and George Washington. When Rachel left her Danish husband, Lavien, she led for a while a very free and easy life and paid a brief visit to the British island of Barbados in 1756. Hamilton was supposedly born in January of the following year.

> This raises an interesting question. Washington was on Barbados in 1756. Washington's devotion to Hamilton was so marked that their enemies spread the story that they were father and son. What foundation they thought they had for this particular bit of scandal is unrecorded. Lavine [Lavien] specifically states that Rachel was on Barbados in 1756.[1]

[1] Gertrude Atherton, *Adventures of a Novelist* (New York, 1932), pp. 353-353. See also Gertrude Atherton, "The Hunt for Hamilton's Mother," *North American Review*, CLXXV (1902), 229 ff.

Despite Mrs. Atherton's arduous investigations, she is demonstrably mistaken in her statements about Washington. He paid a visit to Barbados in 1752, not 1756, and Hamilton was born in 1755 and not in 1757. Mrs. Atherton was incorrect in some of her other dates and facts as well. Rachel Faucette, Hamilton's mother, was the daughter of John Faucette (or Fawcett), who had emigrated from France to the island of Nevis in 1685. After a brief period of study under a loyal physician, he branched out for himself and soon made a fortune that enabled him to buy a plantation which he called Gingerland. According to one version, Dr. Fawcett married twice. Of the second wife little is known except that her first name was Mary. There is no doubt that the Doctor was many years older than Mary, and he viewed with open dismay the birth in 1729 of a daughter, Rachel.

In February, 1740, the Fawcetts separated, and Mary was legally awarded an annual income of £53 in lieu of any dower claims. In 1745 John died, and in his will all of his estate was left to Rachel, who was named as the executrix. Mary and Rachel now left Nevis and settled on the island of St. Croix. Near at hand was a Danish Jew whose name appears on several documents under variant spellings—Lavien, Lewin, and Lavion. (Mrs. Atherton used the spelling *Lavine.*) It seems probable that sometime in 1745 Rachel, at the age of sixteen, married John Michael Lavien, and went to live on a plantation pleasantly named Contentment.

But what's in a name? Rachel did not find that life with Mr. Lavien spelled *contentment,* no matter how she tried. She was many years younger than her husband, and her blood wanted adventure while his merely yearned for repose and a comfortable spot by the fireside. So while her husband dozed in quiet contentment, Rachel kept nocturnal trysts with many men who were eager to teach her how to answer properly the hot call of the Caribbean. Mr. Lavien had learned the lessons of life in Copenhagen, where life was lived at a slower and more leisurely cadence.

After Rachel had given birth to a son, Peter Lavien, in 1746, her nocturnal exercises under the warm, bright moon took on a regular pattern that was not to the liking of the matter-of-fact Lavien. Finally he appealed to the police, who decided that the only thing to do with the moonstruck Rachel was to confine her in the jail in Christiansted. It is not recorded whether, in order to relieve the tedium of jail life, the conventional warden of the jail incarcerated several young men as companions for Rachel.

According to Lavien, Rachel had been "twice guilty of adultery." Hoping that this taste of jail discipline had calmed her flaming passions, he secured her release, but Rachel followed a code of life advocated in later years by Oscar Wilde: "The best way to get rid of a temptation is to yield to it." Mr. Lavien had a different code of life, and was so shocked by Rachel's behavior that he sued for divorce. According to his complaint, Rachel had "shown herself to be shameless, rude and ungodly," and had given herself up "to whoring with everyone." He was especially anxious to secure a divorce because if he died Rachel, as his widow, might claim for her "whore-children" what really belonged to his legitimate son.[2] The court decided

[2] Broadus Mitchell, *Alexander Hamilton* (New York, 1957-1962, 2 vols.), 6-7. See also Harold Larson, "Alexander Hamilton: The Fact and the Fiction of His Early Years," *William and Mary Quarterly*, IX (3rd series, 139-151, and Harold Larson, "The Birth and Parentage of Alexander Hamilton," *American Genealogist*, XXI, 161-167.

that Lavien had proved his charges against Rachel, and the divorce was granted. Lavien was free to marry again, but his majesty reserved the right to Rachel.

Rachel's next love affair was equally unlucky. She began to live with a James Hamilton some time in 1752. Of Hamilton we know little except that he came from a long line of Hamiltons who in Scotland were gentry of some consequence but whom hard times had followed like a shadow. This financial shadow never left them. As Alexander once remarked about his father's background, "My father's affairs at a very early day, went to wreck," [3] a picturesque phrase that correctly described the family finances.

Rachel, with her two illegitimate sons, James and Alexander, lived alternately on the islands of Nevis, St. Kitts, and St. Croix. In the spring of 1765 Hamilton brought his small family to St. Croix and then largely disappeared from their lives. Rachel's relatives on St. Croix had also fallen upon evil days financially, so she was compelled to rely upon her own efforts to support her family. She rented a small house in Christiansted and opened a store where she sold provisions and plantation supplies. Alexander, then ten years old, helped wait on customers and had his first experience in bookkeeping. Their modest manner of living is shown by the small estate his mother left upon her death.

Alexander was only thirteen years old when his mother died. His relatives on St. Croix were in serious financial straits and could do little to help the orphans. His older brother James was apprenticed to a carpenter, and Alexander was placed in the "counting house" of Beckman and Cruger. His early proficiency in writing and bookkeep-

[3] Quoted in Mitchell, *op. cit.*, I, 9.

ing is something of a mystery, as is his ability to write in French. Indeed, little is known of his formal education, and it appears that he was largely self-taught.

In the commercial establishment of Beckman and Cruger, emphasis was placed upon the export of island products, especially raw sugar, and the importation of supplies for the 380-odd plantations. During Hamilton's clerkship with the firm (1768-1772), the business dealings were largely with Nicholas Cruger's father, uncle, and brothers resident in New York.

The story of Hamilton's clerkship is told in some seventy letters in the Hamilton collection in the Library of Congress.[4] They give a detailed story of the commercial dealings with the American continent of an important firm in Christiansted, and they show Hamilton's exceptional ability in business matters. But his thoughts were not always on the affairs of the counting house. He found time to write a pastoral poem whose first verse ran as follows:

> In yonder mead my love I found
> Beside a murm'ring brook reclin'd:
> Her pretty lambkins dancing round
> Secure in harmless bliss.
> I bad the waters gently glide,
> And vainly hush'd the heedless wind,
> Then, softly kneeling by her side,
> I stole a silent kiss.[5]

---

[4] Many of these letters are published in Alexander Hamilton, *Papers, 1768-1788*, ed. Harold C. Syrett (New York, 1961, 4 vols.), I, 8-34.
[5] *Ibid.*, I, 6-7.

A HURRICANE BLOWS HAMILTON TO AMERICA

His hours of leisure away from his work in the counting house Alexander spent in the company of a Presbyterian clergyman, Hugh Knox, who shaped his mind and gave him the inspiration to move up in the world. Knox had studied several years in the College of New Jersey at Princeton and had taken two degrees there. He was a good classical scholar and had a taste for literature that he imparted to his young protégé. His sermons made a deep impression upon Alexander and were responsible for the youthful piety that strongly colored his early writings. This is especially noticeable in his description of the hurricane that visited St. Croix on August 31, 1772, with devastating force. A paragraph from this description, which was published on October 3 in the *Royal Danish-American Gazette*, gives a good idea of the turgid style that Alexander, then seventeen, affected:

It began about dusk . . . and raged very violently till ten o'clock. . . . Meanwhile, the wind was shifting round to the South West point, from whence it returned with redoubled fury and continued so 'till near three o'clock in the morning. Good God! What horror and destruction. Its impossible for me to describe or you to form any idea of it. It seemed as if a total dissolution of nature was taking place. . . . A great part of the buildings throughout the Island are levelled to the ground, almost all the rest very much shattered. . . . My reflections and feelings on this frightful and melancholy occasion, are set forth in the following self-discourse.

Where now, Oh! vile worm, is all thy boasted fortitude

and resolution? What is become of thine arrogance and
self sufficiency? Why does thou tremble and stand aghast?
How humble, how helpless, how contemptible you now
appear. . . . Oh! impotent presumptuous fool! how durst
thou offend that omnipotence, whose nod alone were sufficient to quell the destruction that hovers over thee, or
crush thee into atoms? . . . Despise thyself, and adore
God.[6]

This bombastic description is hardly the remarkable
performance over which many of his biographers have
gushed so rapturously. But it was good enough to impress
deeply many of Alexander's friends on St. Croix, who followed the urgings of Hugh Knox and contributed enough
money to send the brilliant young man to the North
American continent for extended study. He probably
reached Boston sometime in October, 1772, and soon
moved to New York, where the friendly kin of Nicholas
Cruger made him welcome. But his closest friend in New
York was an emigrant from the north of Ireland with the
portentous name of Hercules Mulligan, who took Alexander under his wing and helped him in innumerable ways.

It was not long before Alexander was sent to Elizabethtown, New Jersey, where he was enrolled in an excellent
academy under a College of New Jersey headmaster. He
soon became acquainted with Elias Boudinot and William Livingston, who were friends of Hugh Knox. Thus
he was fortunate to move in a select circle of outstanding
young Americans whose social connections were of im-
mense value to a young immigrant with little to recom-
mend him but unusual mental agility and charm of manner. Some of the members of this circle became lifetime

[6] *Ibid.*, I, 35-36. This description was in the form of a letter which
Hamilton addressed to his father on September 6, 1772.

friends: William Alexander, later called Lord Stirling because of his claim to a Scottish title; William Duer, later Hamilton's first assistant in the treasury; and John Jay, a budding American statesman who married Sarah Livingston and rose to prominence as a leading member of the Federalist Party.

After a year of diligent study in the academy at Elizabethtown, Hamilton paid a visit to the College of New Jersey to talk with Dr. Witherspoon, but his insistence upon fixing his own rate of progress was not acceptable to the trustees. He then made a visit to King's College in New York City, where his desires received a more friendly hearing.

WAR INTERRUPTS A COLLEGE EDUCATION

In King's College Hamilton met some congenial students with whom he made lasting friendships: Samuel and Henry Nicoll, Nicholas Fish, and Robert Troup. They organized a club of which Hamilton became the leader, and they lengthily debated the issues of the day. Opposition to arbitrary imperial taxation was often developed, and Hamilton followed the line of reasoning frequently expressed by Hugh Knox, who was an ardent defender of colonial rights. His fluency was highly praised, and he was led to send some articles to *Holt's Journal* which attracted wide attention. In a letter to a friend, John Jay remarked: "I hope Mr. Hamilton continues busy. I have not received Holt's paper these three months, and therefore cannot judge of the progress he makes." [7]

[7] Quoted in Nathan Schachner, *Alexander Hamilton* (New York, 1957), p. 32.

On July 6, 1774, Hamilton made a fiery speech at a gathering sponsored by the Sons of Liberty, but he was keeping his mind on his studies and duly registered in King's College for the fall term. The list of books he read in the school library is staggering. This reading stood him in good stead when he prepared a long and cogent reply to a pamphlet written by Dr. Samuel Seabury entitled "Free Thoughts on the Proceedings of the Continental Congress." Hamilton's pamphlet of rebuttal, dated December 15, 1774, bore the title "A Full Vindication of the Measures of Congress," and it was a very serious affair.[8]

But this was only the beginning. Mr. Seabury thought that Hamilton's anonymous pamphlet needed a prompt reply, and countered with a blast entitled "A View of the Controversy." Hamilton hastily answered with a counterblast, "The Farmer Refuted." [9] From weight alone it must have crushed Mr. Seabury—it ran more than eighty pages and contained no froth.

After another pamphlet, "Remarks on the Quebec Bill," Hamilton became immersed in activities connected with drilling and the manual at arms. He belonged to a company of students who wore gaudy uniforms and went through military exercises in the churchyard of St. George's Chapel. As a sequel to one of these daily drills, he helped to drag away some cannon from the battery which the captain of the British warship *Asia* suddenly decided to add to the complement of his ship. During a broadside from the *Asia*, Hamilton "exhibited the greatest unconcern," even when solid shot and musket balls made martial music designed to promote the quick step.

In January, 1776, the New York Provincial Congress de-

[8] See Hamilton, *op. cit.*, I, 45-78.
[9] See *Ibid.*, I, 81-165.

cided to raise a company of artillery for purposes of defense. In March Congress ordered that "Alexander Hamilton, be, and he is hereby appointed Captain of the Provincial Company of the Artillery of this Colony." [10] He had hardly received this appointment when the British army under Lord Howe made a determined thrust at Washington's fortifications on Long Island, turning Washington's left flank, and if Howe had not called back his victorious troops for an early encampment, the result might have been disastrous for the American cause. Washington's masterly retreat from Long Island, then across New Jersey gave him a good opportunity to size up Hamilton's military qualities and led to the young man's appointment as a member of Washington's staff.

In this position his services were invaluable. The communications that came to Washington's headquarters were enormous in bulk. Orders of every kind and correspondence in every category were handed in outline form to Hamilton, whose facile pen translated them into terse, clear, graceful English. It was exhausting work that gave him little opportunity to win any special commendation from his military superior. He chafed at this situation, and finally his impatience boiled over in an outburst that put an end to his clerical duties.

HAMILTON PLACES CUPID HIGH ABOVE MARS

In the midst of the tumult and excitement of war, Hamilton nursed thoughts of marriage. When he finally surrendered his heart it was not to some unknown Maud Miller raking hay in some modest field but to the daughter of an

[10] Quoted in Mitchell, *op. cit.*, I, 79-80.

important Dutch patroon who had a vast estate on the Hudson River, Philip Schuyler. There were four great families in New York at the time of the Revolution—the Van Rensselaers, the Van Cortlandts, the Livingstons, and the Schuylers. Philip Schuyler was a member of a family that had long been comfortably settled in one of the seats of the mighty in the rich farmlands around Albany, and marriage with one of his daughters would give the bridegroom assurance of important family connections and a reasonable amount of wealth. Schuyler himself had sided with the American cause from the outbreak of the Revolution, and in the army had risen to the rank of major general. He was distinctly a person of importance.

His daughter Elizabeth, or Betsey, had sufficient good looks and charm to attract the eyes of young military officers in the Continental Army. One of them, Tench Tilghman, made a colorful entry in his journal after meeting her on August 22, 1775: "I was prepossessed in favor of this young Lady the moment I saw her. A Brunette with the most good natured lively dark eyes that I ever saw, which threw a beam of good temper and benevolence over her whole Countenance." [11]

Hamilton probably met Betsey Schuyler through the good offices of Catharine Livingston. This is the same lass who flirted with Gouverneur Morris and evoked from him some wretched poetry but also some letters which gave early evidence that he was a writer of promise. Apparently, Kitty Livingston and Betsey Schuyler were interested in attending a dance to be given in Morristown, and they made overtures to Hamilton for a safe escort. The answering note, dated February, 1780, shows that he was familiar

[11] Tench Tilghman, *Memoirs,* ed. Oswald Tilghman (Albany, 1876), pp. 89 ff.

with the turn of phrase expected from gallant young officers who had been asked to do a favor for desirable
young ladies:

> Col. Hamiltons compliments to Miss Livingston and
> Miss Schuyler. He is sorry to inform them that his zeal
> for their service makes him forget that he is so bad as a
> Charioteer as hardly to dare to trust himself with so
> precious a charge; though if he were only to consult his
> own wishes like Phaeton he would assemble the chariot of
> the sun, if he were sure of experiencing the same fate.
> Col. Tilghman offers himself a volunteer.[12]

It is certain that Colonel Tilghman was an eager volun-
teer to act as an escort to the young lady whose beauty
and charm had made such an indelible impression upon
him back in 1775. It would be his last service in this regard; Hamilton now began to press his suit in earnest, and
he wished no more volunteers to make offers of assistance.
He began by way of indirection. In a letter to Margarita
Schuyler in February he confessed that he had been
caught in a web of attraction that Betsey had woven
round him:

> I have already confessed the influence your sister has
> gained over me; yet notwithstanding this, I have some
> things of a very serious and heinous nature to lay to her
> charge. She is most unmercifully handsome and so per-
> verse that she has none of those pretty affectations which
> are the prerogatives of beauty. . . . In short she is so
> strange a creature that she possesses all the beauties and
> graces of her sex without any of those amiable defects,
> which from their general prevalence are esteemed by

[12] Hamilton, *op. cit.*, II, 262.

connoisseurs necessary shades in the character of a fine woman. . . . I should never have done, were I to attempt to give you a catalogue . . . of all the hearts she has vanquished.[13]

In the following month Hamilton's love for Betsey grew rapidly warmer, and its heat could be perceived in every paragraph of his letters. He had been told that she planned a trip to Philadelphia, he wrote on March 17. He hoped soon to return to Morristown, and her presence there would be ineffably sweet. But she should not bother too much about his desires:

> I beg too you will not suffer any considerations respecting me to prevent your going; for though it will be a tax upon my love to part with you so long, I wish you to see that city before you return. . . . Only let me entreat you to endeavour not to stay there longer than the amusements of the place interest you, in complaisance to friends; for you must always remember your best friend is where I am. If possible and you give me your consent I should try to make a short visit to the city while you are there. . . .
>
> I had written so far when the express arrived with your dear billet under cover of one from your guardian. I cannot tell you what extacy I felt in casting my eye over the sweet effusions of tenderness it contains. My Betseys soul speaks in every line and bids me be the happiest of mortals. I am so and will be so. You give me too many proofs of your love to allow me to doubt it and in the conviction that I possess that, I possess everything the world can give.[14]

[13] *Ibid.*, II, 169-170.
[14] *Ibid.*, II, 285-287.

Hamilton now took up with General Schuyler the serious matter of marriage with his daughter Elizabeth. The General promptly wrote Hamilton (April 8) and indicated his wife's consent to such a union, but he thought the *"dernier pas"* should be postponed a while. He expected to be in "camp in a few days when we will adjust all matters." [15] Hamilton wrote Mrs. Schuyler on April 14 to thank her for her consent to the marriage: "I leave it to my conduct rather than expressions to testify the sincerity of my affection for her, the respect I have for her parents, the desire I shall always feel to justify their confidence and merit their friendship." [16]

These letters of Hamilton were written with an ardor and affection that seemed entirely genuine, and both Betsey and her parents had no doubt about that fact. But apparently Hamilton, like some men, had two hearts, one on his sleeve for surface lovemaking and one he reserved for weightier affairs. In a letter from Betsey's warm admirer Tench Tilghman to his brother William, some sentences reveal that even while Hamilton was writing these passionate letters to Betsey, he was also making warm advances to a girl named Polly:

Alas poor Polly! Hamilton is a gone man, and I am too old for his substitute—She had better look out for herself and not put her trust in Man. She need not be jealous of the little Saint [a reference to Betsey's piety]. She is gone to Pennsylvania and has no other impressions than those of regard for a very pretty good tempered Girl, the daughter of one of my most valuable acquaintances.[17]

[15] Quoted in *ibid.*, II, 305-306.
[16] *Ibid.*, II, 309-310.
[17] Tilghman, *op. cit.*, p. 173.

Very little is known of Polly and her unfortunate love affair with Hamilton. In Nathan Schachner's biography of Hamilton there is a brief mention of her:

> It would seem Hamilton was seriously entangled right up to the announcement of his engagement. It would also appear that Hamilton's courtship of Eliza had been so discreetly conducted that Polly, a comparative stranger to the Schuylers, though well known to the Tilghmans, left Morristown without the slightest knowledge that she had been displaced in his affections.[18]

With Polly out of the way, Hamilton pursued Betsey with renewed ardor, and felt so certain of his suit that he delicately suggested that she read more widely so as to improve her mind:

> I love you more and more every hour. The sweet softness and delicacy of your mind and manners, the elevation of your sentiments . . . and that innocent simplicity and frankness which pervade your actions; all these appear to me with increasing amiableness and place you in my estimation above all the rest of your sex. I entreat you my Charmer, not to neglect the charges I gave you, particularly that of taking care of yourself, and that of employing all your leisure in reading. . . . You excel most of your sex in all the amiable qualities; endeavour to excel them equally in the splendid ones.[19]

There is no record that Betsey paid the slightest attention to Hamilton's subtle suggestion that she improve her

18 Schachner, *op. cit.,* p. 108.
19 Hamilton, *op. cit.,* II, 350.

mind through wide reading. Her sister Angelica had attended a fashionable seminary in New Rochelle and spoke with more fluency and authority than Betsey. Indeed, some historians have ventured the opinion that Angelica, married to a stodgy businessman, keyed her conversation with Hamilton to a high pitch of wit and repartee that she seldom employed with any other man. They have also harbored the thought that he enjoyed these verbal pyrotechnics, and perhaps that was the reason he quietly suggested to Betsey that she spend her leisure time reading.

But Hamilton did not press this suggestion, and his letters expressed a constant warmth that must have flattered Betsey deeply. "Assure yourself my love," he wrote on July 6, that you are seldom a moment absent from my mind, that I think of you constantly and talk of you frequently. . . . Adieu, my angel, be happy and love me as I love you."[20]

Hamilton felt strong pride of possession in being engaged to Betsey, and it disturbed him very much when she was a little remiss in her correspondence. On July 20, when she was two weeks late in replying to his July 6 letter, he reproached her for neglect:

Pardon me my lovely girl for any thing I may have said that has the remotest semblance of complaining. If you knew my heart thoroughly, you would see it so full of tenderness for you that you would not only pardon, but you would even love my weaknesses. For God's sake my dear Betsey try to write me oftener.[21]

[20] *Ibid.*, II, 353.
[21] *Ibid.*, II, 361.

Three weeks later he returned to this charge of neglect:

> I love you more than I ought—more than is consistent
> with my peace. . . . But why do you not write to me
> oftener? It is again an age since I have heard from you.
> I write you at least three letters for your one, though I
> am immersed in public business and you have nothing to
> do but to think of me.[22]

Late in August, 1780, he continued in the same complaining vein, but he finally struck a bright note about the
possibility that peace was near at hand. In that event an
early marriage could be arranged. But would Betsey be
satisfied to marry an officer in straitened financial circumstances?

> Do you soberly relish the pleasure of being a poor man's
> wife? Have you learned to think a home spun preferable
> to a brocade and the rumbling of a waggon wheel to the
> musical rattling of a coach and six? Will you be able to
> see with perfect composure your old acquaintances flaunt-
> ing it in gay life, tripping it along in elegance and splen-
> dor, while you hold an humble station and have no other
> enjoyments than the sober comforts of a good wife? . . .
> If you cannot my Dear we are playing a comedy . . . and
> you should correct the mistake before we begin the . . .
> tragedy of the unhappy couple.[23]

Betsey answered Hamilton's important questions with a
poem that stressed the fact that her love was not based
upon material wealth but upon the many intangibles
whose importance only the heart may know. It was an
answer that calmed his fears and gave him a deeper un-

[22] *Ibid.*, II, 374-375.
[23] *Ibid.*, II, 397-399.

derstanding of the things that lay closest to Betsey's heart.

In the first week in September, when Hamilton heard of the disastrous defeat of the American army at Camden, he thought that perhaps he and Betsey might have to flee America and settle in Switzerland:[24]

> What have we to do with any thing but Love? Go the world as it will, in each others arms we cannot but be happy. If America were lost we should be happy in some other clime more favourable to human rights. What think you of Geneva as a retreat? 'Tis a charming place.

In the meantime, General Benedict Arnold's treason was discovered. He escaped, but his British accomplice, Major André, was captured and sentenced to be hanged. Arnold's wife, the former Peggy Shippen of Philadelphia, made a dramatic avowal of innocence which deceived a number of American officers, Hamilton among them. We now know that she was deeply involved in the plot to betray Washington into British hands and to arrange for West Point to fall into British possession.[25]

Hamilton was particularly disturbed that Major André was condemned by a court martial to be hanged, and he pleaded in vain with Washington to permit André to be shot instead of having to undergo the humiliation of the gibbet. He confided to Betsey on October 2 that "when André's tale comes to be told, and present resentment is over, the refusing him the privilege of choosing the manner of death will be branded with too much obduracy." [26]

[24] *Ibid.*, II, 418-420.
[25] Carl Van Doren, *The Secret History of the American Revolution* (New York, 1941), pp. 200-201.
[26] Hamilton collection, Library of Congress.

The hazards and trials of war seemed to increase the ardor of Hamilton's affection for Betsey, and his letters reflect this heightened passion. He wrote on October 5:

> I have told you and I told you truly that I love you too much. You engross my thoughts too entirely to allow me to think anything else. You not only employ my mind all day, but you intrude on my sleep. I meet you in every dream and when I wake I cannot close my eyes again for ruminating on your sweetness.[27]

In this letter Hamilton promised to write to Betsey a "particular account of André." In a letter to Lieutenant Colonel John Laurens on October 11 he discussed the André matter in full and sent a copy of the letter to Betsey. It is a detailed story of the conspiracy among Arnold, General Clinton, and André. He told of his visits to confer with André and his high opinion of the gentlemanly qualities of the unfortunate British officer. It is apparent that his sympathy was with André, and he deeply resented Washington's adamant refusal to change the means of execution from hanging to a firing squad.[28] From this time on, "Hamilton was no longer to survey his commander-in-chief with the eyes of unquestioning loyalty; a certain coldness faintly tinged their relations, almost imperceptible at first, but to grow secretly in strength until the final explosion." [29]

This resentment at Washington's treatment of Major André did not find expression in Hamilton's letters to Bet-

27 Hamilton, *op. cit.*, II, 455-456.
28 *Ibid.*, II, 460-470.
29 Schachner, *op. cit.*, p. 119.

sey, which continued in the key of warm passion. He confessed that he was

> . . . too much in love to be either reasonable or witty; I feel in the extreme; and when I attempt to speak of my feelings I rave. I have remarked to you before that real tenderness has always a tincture of sadness, and when I affect the lively my melting heart rebels. It is separated from you and it cannot be cheerful.[30]

When two weeks passed without a letter from Betsey, Hamilton once more reverted to the role of complaining lover. Why the delay in her letters?

> It is now a fortnight since I have received a line from my Charmer; but I attribute it to the interruptions of conveyance. I wish however, you would write by the post, which would ensure me a letter once a week at least. . . . I almost pine after peace. Then if ever I suffer you to be out of my sight, it will be an unwilling sacrifice to decorum. . . . God bless you My Darling girl. . . . Tell all the family I love them, and assure yourself that my affection for you is inviolable.[31]

HAMILTON MARRIES BETSY AND LEAVES THE ARMY

These complaints of a frustrated lover came to an end on December 14, 1780, when Hamilton and Betsey Schuyler were formally married in the First Reformed Church in Albany. The ceremony was followed by a reception in the

---

[30] Hamilton, *op. cit.*, II, 473-474.
[31] *Ibid.*, II, 492-494.

Schuyler mansion. After an extended honeymoon, Hamilton somewhat reluctantly began to think of his military duties. He first wrote to Washington concerning the condition of the armory at Albany. He and Betsey then presented their "respectful compliments" to the commander in chief and his wife. They also conveyed the ardent wish of General Schuyler that the Washingtons find time to visit the Schuyler home.[32]

Hamilton's marriage to a Schuyler heiress had placed him upon a distinctly higher social level. He had now found social and financial security, but he was not satisfied with his position on Washington's staff. After much debate the Continental Congress had adopted his suggestion to remove the administration of national finances from the inept hands of the Committee on Finances and substitute a single, efficient financial officer who could bring order out of the existing chaos. General John Sullivan, now a member of Congress, wrote to Washington on January 29, 1781, with regard to this proposed change in financial administration and requested his opinion "with respect to Colo. Hamilton as a Financier." [33]

Washington was surprised at this communication, and did not seem to realize all its implications. It was only one of a series of letters he had received suggesting another military assignment for Colonel Hamilton or even a diplomatic appointment. He would hate to lose his able staff officer who had been such an efficient secretary, but he allowed none of these misgivings to color his letter to General Sullivan, dated February 4:

[32] December 19, 1780; *ibid.*, II, 524-525.
[33] *Letters of Members of the Continental Congress,* ed. E. C. Burnett (New York, 1921, 8 vols.), V, 548.

How far Colo. Hamilton, of whom you ask my opinion as a financier, has turned his thoughts to that particular study, I am unable to ansr., because I never entered upon a discussion of this point with him. But this I can venture to advance, from a thorough knowledge of him that there are few men to be found, of his age, who have a more general knowledge than he possesses; and none, whose soul is more firmly engaged in the cause, or who exceeds him in probity and sterling virtue.[34]

General Sullivan's efforts were in vain. The Continental Congress selected Robert Morris instead of Hamilton to be superintendent of finance, and Hamilton's hopes were once more frustrated. He began to get definitely edgy, and it took only a minor occurrence to lead to a break with Washington. On February 16, 1781, he was hurrying downstairs in headquarters with an order for the commissary. On the staircase he met Washington who remarked: "I would like to speak with you, Colonel Hamilton." Hamilton replied, "I will wait upon you immediately, sir." But in the hall he met with Lafayette, who detained him for a few moments. When at length he ascended the stairs he found General Washington at the top landing, wearing a frown of annoyance on his face. "Colonel Hamilton," he burst out angrily, "you have kept me waiting at the head of these stairs these ten minutes. I must tell you, sir, you treat me with disrespect." "I am not conscious of it, sir," Hamilton replied with some heat, "but since you have thought it necessary to tell me so, we part."

Washington was plainly surprised at Hamilton's rejoinder. After glancing at him coldly for a moment, he abruptly ended the conversation: "Very well, sir, if it be your

[34] George Washington, *Writings, 1745-1799*, ed. John C. Fitzpatrick (Washington, D.C., 1931-1944, 40 vols.), XXI, 181.

choice." After Hamilton had remained in his room for a while, Washington sent Tench Tilghman, a mutual friend, with an olive branch. Would not Hamilton return to the General's office for a frank conversation in order to clear up all differences? Hamilton brushed aside the proffered olive branch and informed Tilghman that he would remain as a staff officer only until the commander in chief could secure "other assistance by the return of some of the gentlemen who are absent." [35]

Hamilton's version of this breach with Washington is told in a letter he wrote to General Schuyler on February 18. The letter is not to Hamilton's credit. He assured Schuyler that for "three years past I have felt no friendship for him and have professed none." When Washington had made some advances of friendship, Hamilton had repelled them because he wished the General clearly to understand that he wished their relations "to stand rather upon a footing of military confidence than of private attachment." [36]

This letter, which gives its writer the earmarks of an insufferable coxcomb, revealed a side of Hamilton that has deeply disturbed his biographers. But even worse was the letter he wrote on the same day to his intimate friend Major James McHenry:

> The Great man and I have come to an open rupture. Proposals of accomodation have been made on his part but rejected. I pledge my honor to you that he will find me inflexible. He shall for once at least repent his ill-humour. . . . Adieu, my friend. May the time come when characters may be known in their true light.[37]

[35] Schachner, *op. cit.*, pp. 125-127.
[36] Hamilton, *op. cit.*, II, 563-568.
[37] *Ibid.*, II, 569.

This sneering and unjust letter from Hamilton will always remain a blot upon his character, and it defies any satisfactory explanation. After reading Hamilton's letter of February 18, his father-in-law suggested in a February 25 reply that attempts be made to effect a reconciliation. But both Schuyler's and Lafayette's pleading with Hamilton to seek a reconciliation was in vain, and on April 30, 1781, he tendered his formal resignation.

Just before his resignation went into effect, Hamilton wrote Washington and asked to be designated to a command, perhaps to a light corps. This request placed Washington in an embarrassing position, because he had been deluged with complaints from officers who resented being supplanted by new officers who had only a very short period of command experience. He put this matter clearly in a letter to Hamilton, but Hamilton continued to insist upon his request, vehemently asserting that he could see no "insuperable obstacles to a compliance." Finally Washington gave in, and before the siege of Yorktown he gave Hamilton the command post he had asked for with such ill grace.

Hamilton was able to storm a minor redoubt and thus gained the glory that was so dear to his heart. But in his letters to his wife and General Schuyler he made no mention of the unusual courtesies he had received from General Washington. It was far easier for him to criticize his commander in chief than to give him the praise he so justly deserved.[38]

[38] *Ibid.*, II, 682-683.

THE BEGINNINGS OF HAMILTON'S
PUBLIC LIFE

After leaving the army Hamilton went at once to Albany
to await the birth of his first child, a son named Philip
after General Schuyler. He then moved his family to Philadelphia and prepared to enter the legal profession. But
his progress was delayed by his acceptance of the position
of receiver of continental taxes for the state of New York.
The work in connection with this office was exhausting
and the compensation disappointing, but he was brought
into close contact with the members of the legislature.
Through the strong pressure he was able to exert, the legislature was induced to adopt an important resolution
which called for a "Convention of the States to Revise and
Amend the Articles of Confederation." [39]

The legislature went one step farther and voted to
send Hamilton as a delegate to the Continental Congress.
When he assumed his seat in November, 1782, he found
a dispirited, leaderless group of men, many of whom
had not been paid any salary for many months. His letters
from Betsey helped sustain his drooping morale:

> I thank you my beloved for your precious letter by the
> post. It is full of that tender love which I hope will char-
> acterize us both to our latest hour. For my own part I may
> say there never was a husband who could vie with yours
> in fidelity and affection. [40]

[39] *Ibid.*, III, 110-113.
[40] December 18, 1782; *ibid.*, III, 226.

Hamilton fought hard to convince Congress that it was necessary for the national government to have a revised system of taxation that would insure a revenue adequate to national needs. This struggle won the admiration of General Schuyler, who wrote in glowing terms to Betsey: "Hamilton . . . affords me satisfaction too exquisite for expression. . . . He is considered, as he certainly is, the ornament of his country, and capable of rendering it the most essential services." [41]

But Hamilton's efforts were in vain, and in July, 1783, he retired to the practice of law, which he had studied at home. He appeared to be a model husband and father, and his paternal obligations grew apace. On September 25, 1784, Betsey gave birth to a daughter, whom they named Angelica, and she was followed at regular intervals by six more hostages to fortune—Alexander, James Alexander, John Church, William Stephen, Eliza, and finally Philip II. (Philip I was killed in a duel.) It was imperative for Hamilton to be successful in the practice of law.

But he realized that prosperity in New York was largely dependent upon national prosperity, and this would be impossible as long as the national government labored under the disability of the Articles of Confederation. The Constitutional Convention finally met in Philadelphia in May, 1787, and it is to Hamilton's credit that he played a leading part in the movement behind it. He was not a major participant in the debates in the Convention, and little attention was paid to the plan he presented. His important contribution was his successful effort to secure ratification of the Constitution in the New York ratifying convention.

To support the drive for general ratification he pub-

[41] Quoted in Schachner, *op. cit.*, pp. 159-160.

lished, along with Madison and John Jay, a series of articles over the name of Publius which had great influence in molding the minds of a large number of voters in favor of ratification. The first of this series appeared on October 27, 1787, in the *Independent Journal* of New York, and the last appeared nearly a year later, August 15, 1788.[42] These essays were later published as the *Federalist Papers*, with Hamilton writing the largest number of them. Even today they are still regarded as an invaluable contemporary interpretation of the Constitution by outstanding Americans who had an important role in the drafting of that federal frame of government.

But even after the ratification of the Constitution had been completed it was necessary to select for the presidency a representative American who had the vision, courage, and ability to make the new machinery of government work effectively, and Washington was the inevitable choice. The chief executive immediately turned to the task of surrounding himself with a group of able consultants, later called a cabinet. One of the most important members of this Cabinet was the secretary of the treasury. Since 1781 Washington had carefully watched Hamilton at work upon an attempted solution of many national fiscal problems, and in 1789 he confidently chose him as his chief financial adviser. The wisdom of his selection was confirmed by America's remarkable quick passage from financial chaos into a stabilized economy that made future national greatness possible.

[42] These important essays were published in several New York newspapers—the *Independent Journal, New York Packet, Daily Advertiser, New York Journal,* and *Daily Patriotic Register.* An excellent essay on the authorship of the *Federalist Papers,* along with the publication of the papers ascribed to Hamilton's authorship, is contained in Hamilton, *op. cit.,* IV, 287-721.

DIPLOMATIC AND AMOROUS INTRIGUES

It is much to Hamilton's discredit that behind the back of Jefferson, secretary of state in Washington's first cabinet, he carried on diplomatic intrigues that severely injured American interests. After 1787 an unaccredited British observer paid extended visits to Philadelphia to watch the American government in action. This Major Beckwith cultivated an intimacy with Hamilton, who was in spirit a member of "the party of the British interest."

In 1791, partly through Hamilton's influence, proposed commercial legislation aimed at Britain was killed in Congress. Through Hamilton Major Beckwith knew all the behind-the-scenes maneuvers that went on in Congress, and their intimacy was helpful to British interests.[43] The American government had a strong case against Britain for her nonfulfillment of the peace treaty. Knowing of American dissatisfaction on this ground, George Hammond, Britain's first minister to the United States, sent Jefferson a long note in defense of the British position. Jefferson's reply of May 29, 1792, carefully dissected and cogently disproved the burden of Hammond's note; the latter, thoroughly dismayed when he read Jefferson's reply, ran to Hamilton for comfort. In a disreputable manner, Hamilton lamented the "intemperant" violence of Jefferson's note and assured Hammond that it did not reflect "the true sentiments of the Administration."

This statement was a plain lie which adversely affected

[43] See Samuel F. Bemis, "Thomas Jefferson," in Samuel F. Bemis *et al.*, eds., *American Secretaries of State and Their Diplomacy* (New York, 1927-1929, 10 vols.), II, 29-30.

Jefferson's policy. As a matter of fact, Jefferson had submitted his note to Hamilton for comments and then had given it to Washington with Hamilton's notes. Washington thoroughly sanctioned the position taken by Jefferson.

Hamilton's conduct in connection with the Jay Treaty was similarly reprehensible. After John Jay had journeyed to London and had drawn from the British foreign secretary the outline of a treaty which he thought was acceptable, Hamilton, once more in his backstairs diplomacy, injured American interests in a vital manner. Britain was fearful that the American government might accept an invitation to become a member of the Armed Neutrality (Russia, Sweden, and Denmark) which was exerting pressure upon Britain in favor of more liberal principles of international law. This fear became a moderating influence upon British policy toward the United States. But Hamilton, in a statement to Hammond in Philadelphia, discounted these fears and assured him that "It was the settled policy of this Government . . . to avoid entangling itself with European connexions which could only tend to involve this country in disputes wherein it might have no possible interest."

With fears of American membership in the Armed Neutrality dissolved, the British foreign secretary now boldly insisted upon a treaty which was bitterly condemned by large groups in the United States. Once again Hamilton, by dubious diplomatic methods, had adversely affected the progress of Anglo-American relations. Professor Dice R. Anderson remarks: "As Hamilton had attempted to overreach Jefferson, and was overreaching Randolph, so he succeeded in overreaching Jay and the interests of his country." [44]

[44] Dice R. Anderson, "Edmund Randolph," in *ibid.*, II, 136.

The split in Hamilton's loyalties was not limited to affairs of state. In an able portrait of Hamilton in his well-known work *Jefferson and Hamilton,* Claude G. Bowers makes an interesting remark: "His one serious weakness was an inordinate fondness for women." [45] It was a weakness, as we have seen, that was shared by a number of our founding fathers.

But the women who had fascinated Washington, Franklin, Jefferson, and Gouverneur Morris had possessed both beauty and brains, and in France Morris's mistress was a person of culture who became a famous novelist. The woman who attracted Hamilton's attention in 1791 had no claim to culture, and her letters to him reveal her to have been a person of neither education nor refinement. Maria Reynolds was a brazen hussy with a strong penchant for sex who seemed to set Hamilton's nerves on urge. There is no portrait of her and no contemporary description. Nathan Schachner wrote of her "coarsely handsome features," [46] while Hamilton's grandson called her a "coarse and illiterate woman," and expressed surprise that a person of Hamilton's distinction could have been "led into an amour" with a woman who had no morals and no social position. Such an entanglement could "only be understood by those who are familiar with the sporadic lapses upon the part of other great men." [47] Bowers, in discussing this scandal, came to the comforting conclusion that Mrs. Reynolds must have been "comely." [48] Other-

[45] Claude G. Bowers, *Jefferson and Hamilton* (New York, 1925), p. 38.

[46] Schachner, *op. cit.,* p. 367.

[47] Allan M. Hamilton, *The Intimate Life of Alexander Hamilton* (London, 1910), p. 60.

[48] Bowers, *op. cit.,* p. 188.

wise, Hamilton's conduct is beyond any rational explanation.

His affair with Mrs. Reynolds began in the summer of 1791 when she called at his residence and asked to speak to him in private. She was wearing a well-fitted garment which set off such attractive contours that Hamilton was glad to invite her in for a quiet conference. After a brief period of convulsive sobbing, Maria told him that her husband had deserted her for another woman, leaving her destitute. She hoped that Hamilton would provide her with funds to return to her friends in New York City.

Mrs. Reynolds had been carefully coached by her husband to make this moving plea to Hamilton and to endeavor to lure him to her bedroom where she could stage the first act of a blackmail scheme. As an actress she played her role to perfection. Her sultry beauty, combined with sexual charm he had seldom encountered, seems to have made his warm Caribbean blood come to a sudden boil. He told her that her "situation was a very interesting one" and he was disposed to help her. But he had no funds with him. If she would leave her address, he would call at her room and give her the money.

Maria knew at once that her plan had succeeded. Hamilton was one of the most important officials in Philadelphia. For him to leave his mansion secretly at night to have a rendezvous with her meant that she had moved him so deeply he was casting discretion to the winds. She hurried to her room to make ready for the most important seduction of her life. She was an expert at this game, but she had never played it for such high stakes.

Late that night Hamilton called at her house and asked for Mrs. Reynolds. When he was shown to her room, he promptly thrust into her hand a bank bill he was sure she wanted. In her scanty attire she looked particularly attractive. Her eyes were big and blue and looked a good deal like a banker's briefcase—replete with promissory notes. Hamilton immediately took one, and she paid it with such warm interest that he must have decided that Maria was the eternal Eve and that the Garden of Eden had suddenly been moved to Philadelphia.[49]

Betsey unwittingly helped the situation for Maria by taking the children to Albany for a long vacation. It was now possible for Hamilton to arrange "frequent meetings" with Maria at his own home, and he thus dishonored the bed customarily shared with Betsey. Passion was so dominant that Hamilton disregarded the fact that these frequent visits to his house at night might be noticed by some of his numerous enemies and lead to a scandal that could threaten his career.

During one rendezvous at Hamilton's house, Maria announced that her husband desired a reconciliation with her. Hamilton urged her to accept a reconciliation and at their next meeting she informed him that this arrangement had been completed. She then hinted that her husband knew of some dubious speculations that were being carried on by certain employees in the Treasury Department.

Reynolds then appeared at Hamilton's office and declared that William Duer, before his resignation from the department, had given him a list of claims against the Treasury. Hamilton pretended an interest in Reynolds' statements and asked some leading questions. Reynolds then paid a second visit to Hamilton's office and requested an appointment to the Treasury. Hamilton admitted in his

[49]Alexander Hamilton, *Works,* ed. H. C. Lodge (New York, 1903, 12 vols.), VII, 388-389.

narrative on the affair that he felt it was in "the interest of my passions" to arrange for a clerkship. He also stated that his relations with Mrs. Reynolds would "naturally incline me to conciliate this man and I might have used vague words which raised expectations." In the end he decided that want of character on Reynolds' part would make it dangerous to give him employment. When Hamilton told Reynolds that there was no vacancy at the time in the Treasury, he turned him into a dangerous enemy who later greatly embarrassed him.

Despite the fact that Hamilton had rejected Reynolds' request, the intrigue with Mrs. Reynolds continued. Hamilton admitted that "various reflections induced me to wish a cessation" of his relations with Maria, but his desires overcame his will. When he weakly intimated to Maria that he would have to stop seeing her, she became distraught and showed "all the appearances of violent attachment and of agonizing distress at the idea of a relinquishment." In the face of such passionate love, how could he possibly break up the affair? Of course, he did owe fidelity to Betsey, who loved him devotedly, but he would soon get over this madness and things would return to normal. In the meantime perhaps he could adopt a plan of "gradual discontinuance rather than of sudden interruption." But Maria's own passion would not be satisfied with the formula of "once-in-a-while," and she sent him a number of "pathetic effusions" which showed unmistakably that she was "truly fond" of him.

One of the letters which he called "pathetic effusions" came to him on December 15, 1791. His affair with Maria had already lasted six months, and no demand for money had yet been made; but Reynolds was now ready to begin blackmailing. The first notes were sounded by Maria in an illiterate letter to Hamilton:

> I have not tim to tell you the cause of my present troubles only that Mr. has rote you this morning and I do not know wether you have got the letter. . . . he has swore that If you do not answer It or If he dose not se or hear from you to day he will write Mrs. Hamilton he has just Gone oute and I am a Lone I think you had better come her one moment that you May know the Cause then you will the better know how to act Oh my God I feel more for you than myself and wish I had never been born to give you so mutch unhappiness do not rite to him no not a Line but come her soon do not send or leave any thing in his power.[50]

On this same day, December 15, a letter came to Hamilton from James Reynolds, who began to play the part of an outraged husband. It was written in the same illiterate style that characterized Maria's letter, and its contents must have given Hamilton some uneasy moments. Fortunately, Betsey had suspected nothing. In this regard Hamilton was one of the most ambidextrous statesmen in American history: with one hand he could pass out blackmail payments to the husband of his mistress, and with the other he could write passionate love letters to Betsey. On July 27, 1791, after she had left for Albany, he wrote her a note which ended in his usual affectionate manner: "Adieu my precious Wife. Blessings without number on you and my little ones." [51]

The letter from Reynolds contained warm complaints

---

50 Quoted in *ibid.*, VII, 423.
51 Quoted in Mitchell, *op. cit.*, II, 400.

about the way Hamilton had seduced his wife. He had arrived home one day and found his wife in tears. It appears that she was often in tears, but on previous occasions she had always had a glib explanation ready:

She always told me that she had bin Reding, and she could not help Crying when she Red any thing that was Afecting, but seing her Repeatedly in that Setevation gave me some suspicion to think that was not the Cause, as fortain would have it. before matters were carred to two great a length, I discovered a letter directed to you which I copied of and put it in the place where I found it without being discovered by Her. and then the evening after, I was Curious enough to watch her. and see give a leter to a Black man in Market Street, which I followed him to your door. after that I Returned home some time in the evening, and I broached the matter to her and Red the Copy to her which she fell upon knees and asked forgiveness and discovered every thing to me Respecting the matter and ses that she was unhappy. and not knowing what to do without some assistance. She called on you for the lone of some money. which you toald her you would call on her the Next Evening which accordingly you did and there Sir you took advantage of a poor Broken harted woman. instead of being a Friend. You have acted the part of the most Cruelist man in existence. You have made a whole family miserable.

She ses there is no other man that she Care for in this world. now Sir you have bin the Cause of Cooling her affections for me. . . . now I am determined to have satisfaction. it shant be onely one family thats miserable. . . . I am determined to leve her and take my daughter with me. . . . now Sir if I Cant see you at your house call and see me. for there is no person that Knowes any thing as yet. . . . put it to your own case and Reflect one moment.

that you should know shush a thing of your wife. would
not you have satisfaction yes. And so will I before one day
passes me more.[52]

On December 19 Reynolds finally came to the point.
His wife's affair with Hamilton had been going on for six
months, and not one cent had been paid for all those
stolen sweets. Something would have to be done about
that right away:

> I have Considered on the matter Serously. I have this
> preposial to make to you. give me the Sum of thousand
> dollars and I will leve the town and take my daughter with
> me and go where my Friend Shant here from me and leve
> her to Yourself to do for her as you thing proper. I hope
> you wont think my request is in a view of making me Sat-
> isfaction for the injury done me. For there is nothing that
> you Can do will compensate for it.[53]

Hamilton thought over this blackmail note very carefully. Up to this point his relations with Maria had cost
him nothing. If he made a payment to the husband now
he would probably have to pay more blackmail in the future; but Maria's charms were worth a great deal to him.
On December 22 he paid Reynolds the sum of $600, and
on January 3, 1792, he turned over to Reynolds an additional sum of $400. He was caught in the meshes of an old
blackmail treadmill and he had no desire to get off. He was
even willing to make more payments to continue a relationship that could easily mean disaster. On January 17
Reynolds assumed the role of procurer for his wife, who
seemingly could not live without Hamilton's loving minis-

[52] Quoted in Hamilton, *Works*, VII, 423-425.
[53] Quoted in *ibid.*, VII, 427-428.

trations. Maria then wrote a note she was certain would speed Hamilton to her bed right away:

> I thought you had been told to stay away from our house and yesterday with tears I my Eyes I beged Mr. once more to permit your visits and he told upon his honnour that he had not said anything to you and that It was your own fault. believe me I scarce knew how to beleeve my senses and if my seturation was insupportable before I heard this It was now more so fear prevents my saing more only that I shal be miserable till I se you and if my dear freend has the Least Esteeme for the unhappy Maria whos greateest fault Is Loveing him he will come as soon as he shall get this and till that time My breast will be the seate of pain and woe.[54]

When Hamilton did not rush to see his "unhappy Maria," she sent another note wet with her tears:

> The girl tells me that you said if I wanted any thing that I should write this morning alas my friend what can ask for but peace wich you alone can restore to my tortured bosom and do My dear Col hamilton on my kneese. Let me Intreatee you to read my Letter and Comply with my request tell the bearer of this or give her a line you need not be the least affraid let me not die with fear have pity on me my freend for I deserve it.[55]

These hysterical letters from Maria acted as a magnet to Hamilton, who could not resist her moving appeals. If he had been a young man in the first flush of manhood his lack of resistance could be understood, but he was now

[54] Quoted in *ibid.*, VII, 430.
[55] Quoted in *ibid.*, VII, 431.

nearing fifty years of age and had heavy marital responsi-
bilities. At home his large family was proof that he did not
neglect the demands of an affectionate wife. His affair
with Mrs. Reynolds showed clearly that he had an excess
of virility that could only delight women with strong passions. In her relations with Hamilton, Maria often sought
sexual satisfaction rather than money. As he remarked
about her behavior the first time he called at her house:
"It was quickly apparent that other than pecuniary consolation would be acceptable." [56]

Most of Hamilton's biographers make light of the Reynolds affair and emphasize its political repercussions. As a
matter of fact, it is the most scandalous love story connected with any of the founding fathers. It was not just a
passing thing; it lasted many months at a high pitch. And
it indicated that Hamilton was a remarkable actor who
could play to perfection the role of upright and loving
husband while secretly trafficking with a woman of no
virtue—and her vermin of a husband.

After more months passed by with Hamilton's usual
nocturnal visits to Mrs. Reynolds' very comfortable bed,
James Reynolds wrote Hamilton a long letter of complaint. What he now did not like was the fact that Hamilton was apparently an expert lover who knew all the tricks
in this important trade. After one of his visits Reynolds
always found his wife in high spirits—"Cheerful and
kind"—but when she had to depend upon her husband as
a lover she was "quite the Reverse." [57]

Hamilton continued to occupy first place in Maria's affections, and soon afterward she wrote another one of her
torrid notes to him:

[56] Quoted in *ibid.*, VII, 427.
[57] March 24, 1792; quoted in *ibid.*, VII, 431-432.

I take up the pen but alas I know not what I write or
how to give you an idea of the anguish wich at this moment rends my heart yes my friend I am doomed to drink
the bitter cup of affliction Pure and unmixed. . . . Oh
merciful God forgive me and you my friend Comply with
this Last Request Let me once more se you and unbosom
Myself to you perhaps I shal be happier after it. I have
mutch to tell wich I dare not write And which you ought
to know. . . . Come therefore to-morrow sometime or Els
in the Evening do I beg you to come gracious God had I
the world I would lay It at your feet If I could only se you
oh I must or I shall lose my senses. . . . dear Col Hamilton . . . when I se you I will do just as you tell me so
doant be offended with me for pleading so hard to se
you.[58]

Hamilton was too softhearted to turn down such a plea
from Maria, especially when she promised to do anything
he wished. But the husband was still intent upon collect-
ing blackmail. On April 3, 1792, James Reynolds made a
request for a "loan of about thirty dollars," and four days
later he sent another note asking for "45 dollars." [59] After
advancing loans to the amount of $165, Hamilton suddenly
received a message on May 2 forbidding him to visit
Mrs. R. any more." [60] But Maria could not stand such pri-
vation, and on June 2 sent him a note to disregard her husband's instructions: "For heaven sake keep me not In suspince Let me know your Intention Either by a Line or
Catline." [61]

Hamilton was not disposed to keep Maria "In suspince,"
and he continued his visits with resulting blackmail. At

[58] N.d.; quoted in *ibid.*, VII, 433-434.
[59] Quoted in *ibid.*, VII, 434-435.
[60] Quoted in *ibid.*, VII, 437-438.
[61] Quoted in *ibid.*, VII, 438.

one time it was $50; another it was $200. Reynolds was putting a high price upon the dubious privilege of sharing his wife's bed, but Hamilton derived such enjoyment out of it that he was willing to be generous. After a series of payments that ran over $1100, the affair was finally terminated in August, 1792.

Apparently Reynolds had often used his wife as attractive bait for wealthy men, but Maria finally rebelled and secured a divorce from him. Her story is told in a letter from Richard Folwell to C. W. Jones. When she had first come to Philadelphia she had been in search of an errant husband who had deserted her. She had discovered that Reynolds had just been liberated from jail and was glad to see her again because he had plans for using her as a prostitute who would "insinuate herself on certain high and influential Characters, endeavour to make Assignations with them, and actually prostitute herself to gull Money from them." [62] When she had tired of him and secured a divorce, she married an equally dubious associate of Reynolds, one Jacob Clingman.

It was inevitable that this unsavory episode in Hamilton's life would be made public. Hamilton had many enemies in Republican ranks, and one of them, John Beckley, a minor Republican politician, was particularly vocal. He had heard some stories from the malodorous Jacob Clingman about speculations in which Hamilton was supposed to be engaged. Beckley turned this information over to James Monroe of Virginia, and Clingman suggested to Monroe that he see James Reynolds for further data.[63] He

[62] A. M. Hamilton, *op. cit.*, p. 210.

[63] It is probable that John Beckley was the person who turned over to James T. Callender the data relating to Hamilton. See Mitchell, *op. cit.*, II, 415-416.

said that Mrs. Reynolds had shown him papers signed by Hamilton which showed that Reynolds had secured from the secretary of the treasury at least $1100 for services rendered—and indeed Reynolds had carefully preserved all of Hamilton's notes to him. Some were unsigned and in an assumed handwriting, but they undoubtedly were from Hamilton and could be used against him.

Egged on by Beckley, Monroe enlisted the interest of two fellow congressmen, Frederick A. Muhlenberg, lately speaker of the House of Representatives, and Abraham Venable, a member of the House. This committee of three began to gather evidence from Clingman and Mrs. Reynolds, and then decided to have an interview with Hamilton and lay the whole matter before him. On December 15, 1792, they called at Hamilton's residence, and when they had presented their evidence he surprised them by revealing the whole story of his relations with Mrs. Reynolds. He was anxious to avoid any breath of scandal with reference to his administration of the Treasury Department. When he completed his story of the Reynolds affair, presenting the pertinent documents, Venable and Muhlenberg were obviously embarrassed and said they had heard enough to clear Hamilton's name of any taint of official misconduct. The documents they had collected and their conversation with Hamilton would be kept secret and confidential.

This pledge of secrecy was kept inviolate until 1797, when James T. Callender published installments of what he termed a *History of the United States for the Year 1796*. Callender was a political scribbler who went through official documents with vacuum-cleaner eyes that picked up mostly dirt. In his first installment he printed the whole story of the charges against Hamilton that had been quietly buried in 1792. Who was responsible for this breach of confidence? Muhlenberg and Venable at once disavowed any complicity in this publication. Monroe kept his silence, even though he had not turned over any data to Callender. When Hamilton faced him in hot anger, a duel was narrowly averted, but this show of belligerence did not bring any new information to light about how this damaging data had found its way to Callender.[64]

With tempers running high and charges and counter-charges filling the air, Hamilton felt that it was imperative for him to place his story before the public. He knew that it would ruin his private reputation and would cause his wife great embarrassment and sorrow, but it would clear his name from the many insinuations that he had been guilty of speculations in public funds while he was secretary of the treasury. He published a pamphlet telling in detail his connection with the Reynoldses.[65]

The public now knew all about Hamilton's lurid love affair with Mrs. Reynolds. It was plain that she had laid a trap which was as old as Eve and had used a bait which has been attractive to men since Adam showed that free will is often on the side of sin. Both Muhlenberg and Venable had talked with Mrs. Reynolds, and after Hamilton's dramatic recital of his relations with her they carefully refrained from chiding him for any moral weakness. The only one who seemed surprised that Hamilton's passion had remained at such a high degree for such a long

---

[64] Schachner, *op. cit.*, 369-371.

[65] Hamilton's pamphlet was entitled, *"Observations on Certain Documents Contained in Nos. V and VI of the History of the United States for the Year 1796, in which the Charge of Speculation Against Alexander Hamilton, late Secretary of the Treasury, is Fully Refuted. Written by Himself."* This pamphlet is printed in full in Hamilton, *Works*, VII, 369-479. It gives a detailed story of the Reynolds affair.

time was Mr. Reynolds, who had watched previous lovers of his wife soon lose interest when the sport led to blackmail. Hamilton's willingness to continue in a game in which he was bound to lose showed there was a certain spark in his blood that he must have inherited from his mother.

As far as blame was concerned, Betsey Hamilton vented most of her anger upon James Monroe, who she was sure had supplied Callender with the documents he had published in his so-called history. She did not denounce her husband, nor did she talk of securing a divorce. She bore her shame in silence, the revelations printed by Callender and by Hamilton himself certainly destroyed some of the pride in and confidence for her husband she had once entertained. She still recognized his superior talents in the fields of finance and politics, but the shadow of marital infidelity, publicly known, darkened her life. She never knew again the glad, confident days she had supremely enjoyed in the first years of her married life.

And Betsey's worries about her flirtatious husband were not entirely over. When her sister Angelica returned to New York in 1797 there were many rumors that Hamilton was too attentive to her. Whether these rumors were true or not, they became damaging to Hamilton's reputation, and it seems that Robert Troup himself believed some of them.[66] According to Claude G. Bowers, "If the ties that bound Angelica Church were not more tender than they should have been, her letters indicate something akin to love." [67] A revealing touch is given in a letter of Harrison Gray Otis to his wife:

[66] Schachner, *op. cit.*, p. 390.
[67] Bowers, *op. cit.*, p. 39.

Tuesday, Dined at Breck's, with Mrs. Church, Miss Schuyler, Genl. Hamilton, Champlin & Mrs. Church, the mirror of affectation, but as she affects to be extremely affable and free from ceremony, this foible is rather amusing rather than offensive. . . . After dinner Mrs. Church dropped her shoe bow, Miss Schuyler picked it up and put it in Hamilton's buttonhole saying 'there brother I have made you a Knight.' 'But of what order' (says Madame Church)? 'He can't be a Knight of the Garter in this company.' 'True sister,' replied Miss Schuyler, 'but he would be *if you would let him.'*

At this same dinner Christopher G. Champlin, a member of Congress from Rhode Island, complained to Otis that Hamilton had cast "some liquorish looks at his cara sposa," and he expressed the opinion that Hamilton appeared "very trifling in his conversation with ladies." Trouble was averted when Champlin's wife assured him that she was not fond of the caster of the "liquorish looks." [68]

John Adams was distinctly critical of Hamilton in this regard, and speaks of his "debaucheries in New York and Philadelphia" and of his "audacious and unblushing attempts upon ladies of the highest rank and purest virtue." [69] To his able and sharp-tongued wife, Abigail, Adams remarked that he knew Hamilton to "be a proud-spirited, conceited, aspiring mortal, always pretending to morality, with as debauched morals as old Franklin who

[68] Samuel E. Morrison, *Life and Letters of Harrison Gray Otis* (Boston, 1913, 2 vols.), I, 141-143.

[69] James Parton, *Life of Aaron Burr* (Boston, 1885, 2 vols.), II, 298.

is more his model than anyone I know. As great an hypocrite as any in the U.S." [70]

John Adams was not telling Abigail a thing. Her sharp
intuition had already told her a great deal about Hamilton. In a reply to her husband, she sharply indicted Hamilton: "Beware of that spare Cassius. . . . . I have read
his heart in his wicked eyes many a time. The very devil is
in them. They are lasciviousness itself." [71]

HAMILTON'S FALLING FORTUNES

Despite the election of John Adams to the presidency in
1796, it was apparent that the power behind the throne
was wielded by Hamilton. Three members of the Adams
cabinet, McHenry, Pickering, and Wolcott, were devoted
to Hamilton and looked to him constantly for direction.
When Talleyrand made the serious mistake of not receiving the commission Adams sent to France to adjust diplomatic difficulties, the reaction in America over the "XYZ
Affair" soon led to a severance of relations. The clouds of
war began to darken the American horizon, and Hamilton
thought it might be an opportune time for him to assume
charge of military preparations if his friends could per-
suade President Adams to give him the chief command.

After Congress had provided the funds for a considerable standing army, Adams sent Secretary of War James
McHenry to Mount Vernon to seek Washington's help and
advice. The former President promptly named Hamilton
as second in command of the proposed army. Considering

[70] Quoted in Page Smith, *John Adams* (Garden City, 1962, 2
vols.), II, 908.
[71] Quoted in *ibid.*, II, 908.

Washington's age, this meant that Hamilton would really be in charge of the military establishment.

But Hamilton's hopes crumbled to nought when President Adams, without consulting his cabinet, sent to the Senate the name of William Vans Murray as minister to France. He had received intimations that Talleyrand wished to avoid war with the United States and would receive Murray in a friendly manner. The treaty of September 30, 1800, promised peace with France; and Hamilton's dreams of military glory and political power, ensured by an effective military machine, quickly faded away.[72]

HAMILTON'S PYRRHIC VICTORY OVER BURR

When President Adams wrecked Hamilton's ambitious military plans, he made a bitter political enemy who was determined to defeat any efforts the President might make to secure a second term. In 1800 Hamilton published a pamphlet bitterly attacking Adams that was as unfortunate as the one he directed against Callender. There were "great and intrinsic defects in his character which unfit him for the office of chief magistrate." He was a man of "disgusting egotism, distempered jealousy, and ungovernable indiscretion" who had tried to overwhelm Mr. Hamilton with a "torrent of gross personal abuse." [73]

Needless to say, by this personal attack upon President Adams, Hamilton had helped to wreck the Federalist Party and make the election of a Democrat almost a cer-

[72] E. Wilson Lyon, "The Franco-American Convention of 1800," *Journal of Modern History*, XII (1940), 305-333; Arthur P. Whitaker, *The Mississippi Question, 1795-1803* (New York, 1934), pp. 115-123.

[73] "*Letter from Alexander Hamilton, Concerning the Public Conduct and Character of John Adams, Esq., President of the United States.*"

tainty. But when Jefferson and Aaron Burr each received 73 electoral votes for President, there was a grave possibility that the election might be thrown into the House of Representatives and that Burr might be returned the victor. To meet this crisis Hamilton now resorted to a letter-writing campaign to his Federalist friends, who were told in stark terms that Burr's "private character is not defended by his most partial friends. He is bankrupt beyond redemption, except by the plunder of his country." He warned Theodore Sedgwick on December 22, 1800, that the election of Burr as President "would disgrace our country abroad. No agreement with him could be relied upon. . . . For heaven's sake, let not the federal party be responsible for the elevation of this man!" [74] Although Hamilton had no use for Jefferson, the famous Virginian was preferable to Burr even though "his politics are tinctured with fanaticism" and despite the fact that "he is a contemptible hypocrite." [75]

After a lengthy period of political manipulation Jefferson was finally chosen as President, but it is significant to note that the twelve New York electoral votes represented the narrow margin by which Adams was defeated. It is particularly important to remember that these electors cast their votes for Democratic candidates only because of Aaron Burr's astute political management, which included the first use of Tammany as a political machine. [76]

Jefferson never forgave Burr for this scare in 1800, and Burr realized that his chances for renomination as Vice

[74] Hamilton, *Works*, X, 397-398.

[75] Hamilton to James A. Bayard, January 16, 1801; *ibid.*, X, 412-419.

[76] See Edward Channing, *History of the United States* (New York, 1917), IV, 237; Charles A. Beard, *Economic Origins of Jeffersonian Democracy* (New York, 1915), pp. 382-387.

President were very slim. He decided to run for the office of governor of New York. Once again Hamilton entered the fight against Burr and tried to divert his Federalist friends from him. At a dinner at the home of Judge John Tayler in Albany, Hamilton was particularly bitter in his remarks about Burr. These trenchant criticisms were conveyed to Burr, who patiently awaited the results of the New York elections. When he lost by a large majority, he sent a letter to Hamilton on June 18, 1804, in which he enclosed a note by Dr. Charles D. Cooper referring to Hamilton's bitter criticisms.

In this regard it is important to observe that Hamilton had long been waging a war of vituperation against persons he did not like. As we have noted, he had recently called President Adams a man of "distempered jealousy" and Jefferson a "contemptible hypocrite." He had almost forced a duel upon James Monroe. This hysterical war of words was bound to cause strong reactions, and he could not have been greatly surprised when he received Burr's letter indicating the "necessity of a prompt and unqualified acknowledgment or denial of the use of any expressions which would warrant the assertions of Mr. Cooper." Accompanying the letter was a newspaper clipping from the Albany *Register* which published the letter from Mr. Cooper citing Hamilton's derogatory remarks.

Hamilton's reply of June 20 was long, rambling, and evasive. He mentioned the fact that most people were familiar with "the animadversions of political opponents upon each other." Burr's reply was sharp and direct: "Political opposition can never absolve gentlemen from the necessity of a rigid adherence to the laws of honour and the rules of decorum. I neither claim such privilege nor indulge it in others." He now required that Hamilton disavow "uttering expressions or opinions derogatory to my honour." The alternative, given the times and the tempers involved, would be a duel.

Hamilton realized that Burr was pushing him to the wall, but he still hoped to postpone the inevitable. He turned to his friend Nathaniel Pendleton for advice, but gained little advantage by this move. On June 22 he wrote another letter to Burr which he must have known would not satisfy Burr's demands. Pendleton held this letter for several days while he and William W. Van Ness, Burr's second, had some useless conversations. On June 25 Van Ness met Pendleton, who handed him Hamilton's explanatory letter of June 22. Hamilton was now trying desperately to stave off a duel. He authorized Pendleton to read to Van Ness a carefully prepared statement that

... in answer to a letter properly adapted ... he [Hamilton] would be able to answer consistently with his honour and truth, in substance, that the conversation to which Doctor Cooper alluded turned wholly on political topics, and did not attribute to Colonel Burr any instance of dishonourable conduct, nor relate to his private character.[77]

When Burr refused to accept this statement as satisfactory, active preparations were made for a duel. On June 27 Van Ness tendered Pendleton Burr's challenge, which was formally accepted, and the duel was arranged for July 11. With a premonition of death, Hamilton wrote a last letter to Betsey on July 10 and exhorted her, in the event of his demise, to "fly to the bosom of your God, and be com-

[77] William Coleman, *A Collection of the Facts and Documents Relative to the Death of Major-General Alexander Hamilton* (New York, 1804; reprinted, Boston, 1904).

forted." [78] In his *apologia* which he wrote in defense of his action in meeting Burr in a duel, he went into some detail:

> It is not to be denied that my animadversions on the political principles, character, and views of Colonel Burr have been extremely severe; and, on different occasions, I, in common with many others, have made very unfavorable criticisms on particular instances of the private conduct of this gentleman. . . . I have resolved . . . to reserve and throw away my first fire, and I have thoughts even of reserving my second fire, and thus give a double opportunity to Colonel Burr to pause and reflect.[79]

Whether at the duel Hamilton actually aimed at Burr and fired his pistol is still a subject of discussion. Hamilton's second, Pendleton, claimed that Hamilton did not fire. Van Ness, Burr's second, was equally positive that Hamilton took aim and actually fired first.[80] In the columns of the *New York Evening Post* and the *Morning Chronicle* this controversy was carried on for some weeks by the seconds, but the dispute generated more heat than light.

Hamilton's death required that his private affairs be closely looked into, and it was discovered that he had not made any money out of his official position as secretary of the treasury. Indeed, he died heavily in debt, which was a melancholy illustration of the fact that the charges brought against him by Reynolds and Clingman were without the slightest foundation. Hamilton had served his country with the same matchless ability that marked the administration of the great British statesman, William Pitt

---

[78] Hamilton, *Works*, X, 475.
[79] Quoted in Mitchell, *op. cit.*, II, 527-528.
[80] Schachner, *op. cit.*, p. 429.

the younger, as the chancellor of the exchequer. Contrary to the case of Pitt, Hamilton's government did not appropriate a large sum of money to liquidate his private debts, a task that confronted his friends for many years after his untimely death.

We shall leave it to other accounts to detail the large debt this country will always owe Hamilton's memory for laying the cornerstone of a financial structure that safely housed our republic for many eventful decades. Our task has been to show that Hamilton was not a man whose head was always full of figures—unless it was the figure of eternal Eve, with all the lore of feminine attraction that may be traced back to the beginning of time.

Selected Bibliography

MANUSCRIPTS AND PRIVATE PAPERS

Franklin, Benjamin: Library of Congress, Washington, D. C.; Pennsylvania Historical Society Archives, Philadelphia, Pennsylvania.

Hamilton, Alexander: Library of Congress, Washington, D. C.

Jefferson, Thomas: Library of Congress, Washington, D. C.; University of Virginia Library, Charlottesville, Virginia.

Morris, Gouverneur: Library of Congress, Washington, D. C.; Massachusetts Historical Society Archives, Boston, Massachusetts.

Washington, George: Library of Congress, Washington, D. C.

PRINTED SOURCES

Adams, Abigail, *Letters of Mrs. Adams, the Wife of John Adams*, ed. C. F. Adams (Boston, 1841, 2 vols.).

Adams, John, *Works, with a Life of the Author by C. F. Adams* (Boston, 1850-1856, 10 vols.).

Franklin, Benjamin, *Benjamin Franklin and Catherine Ray Greene: Their Correspondence, 1755-1790*, ed. William G. Roelker (Philadelphia, 1949).

——, *Papers*, ed. Leonard W. Labaree and Whitfield J. Bell, Jr. (New Haven, 1959-1962, 5 vols.).

——, *Writings*, ed. Albert H. Smyth (New York, 1905-1907, 10 vols.).

Hamilton, Alexander, *Papers, 1768-1788*, ed. Harold C. Syrett (New York, 1961, 4 vols.).

——, *Works*, ed. John C. Hamilton (New York, 1851, 7 vols.).

——, *Works*, ed. H. C. Lodge (New York, 1903, 12 vols.).

Jay, John, *Correspondence and Public Papers*, ed. H. P. Johnston (New York, 1890-1893, 4 vols.).

Jefferson, Thomas, *Correspondence*, with notes by W. C. Ford (Boston, 1916).

——, *Papers*, ed. Julian P. Boyd (Princeton, 1950-1961, 16 vols.).

——, *Writings*, ed. Paul L. Ford (New York, 1892-1899, 10 vols.).

Lee, Richard Henry, *Letters*, ed. James C. Ballagh (New York, 1911-1914, 2 vols.).

Letters of Members of the Continental Congress, ed. E. C. Burnett (New York, 1921, 8 vols.).

Madison, James, *Writings*, ed. Gaillard Hunt (New York, 1900-1910, 9 vols.).

Monroe, James, *Writings*, ed. Stanislaus H. Hamilton (New York, 1898-1903, 7 vols.).

Washington, George, *Letters to Washington and Accompanying Papers*, ed. Stanislaus M. Hamilton (Boston, 1898, 2 vols.).

——, *Writings*, ed. John C. Fitzpatrick (Washington, D. C., 1931-1944, 39 vols.).

AUTOBIOGRAPHICAL SOURCES

Franklin, Benjamin, *Autobiography*, with Introduction by Lewis Leary (New York, 1962).

Gibbs, George, ed., *Memoirs of the Administrations of Washington and John Adams, Edited from the Papers of Oliver Wolcott* (New York, 1846, 2 vols.).

Hamilton, James A., *Reminiscences* (New York, 1896).

Morris, Gouverneur, *A Diary of the French Revolution*, ed. B. C. Davenport (Boston, 1939, 2 vols.).

————, *Diary and Letters* (New York, 1888, 2 vols.).

Tilghman, Tench, *Memoirs*, ed. Oswald Tilghman (Albany, 1876).

Washington, George, *Diaries, 1748-1799*, ed. John C. Fitzpatrick (New York, 1925, 4 vols.).

BIOGRAPHIES

Atherton, Gertrude, *The Conqueror* (New York, 1902).

Beveridge, Albert J., *Life of John Marshall* (New York, 1916, 4 vols.).

Bradford, Gamaliel, *Damaged Souls* (New York, 1931).

Brant, Irving, *James Madison* (Indianapolis, 1941-1953, 4 vols.).

Bruce, William C., *Benjamin Franklin Self-Revealed* (New York, 1942, 2 vols.).

————, *John Randolph of Roanoke, 1773-1833* (New York, 1922, 2 vols.).

Cary, Wilson M., *Sally Cary* (New York, 1916).

Cresson, William P., *James Monroe* (Chapel Hill, 1946).

Fay, Bernard, *Franklin, the Apostle of Modern Times* (New York, 1929).

Fisher, Sydney G., *The True Benjamin Franklin* (Philadelphia, 1899).

Ford, Paul L., *The Many-Sided Franklin* (New York, 1899).

————, *The True George Washington* (Philadelphia, 1896).

Freeman, Douglas S., *George Washington* (New York, 1948, 7 vols.).

Hacker, Louis, *Alexander Hamilton in the American Tradition* (New York, 1957).

Hamilton, Allan M., *The Intimate Life of Alexander Hamilton* (London, 1911).

Hamilton, John C., *Life of Alexander Hamilton* (New York, 1834-1840, 2 vols.).

Hughes, Rupert, *George Washington, the Human Being and the Hero, 1732-1762* (New York, 1926-1929, 2 vols.).

Malone, Dumas, *Jefferson and His Time* (Boston, 1948-1951, 2 vols.).

McMaster, John B., *Benjamin Franklin as a Man of Letters* (Boston, 1887).

Mitchell, Broadus, *Alexander Hamilton* (New York, 1957-1962, 2 vols.).

Monaghan, Frank, *John Jay, Defender of Liberty* (Indianapolis, 1935).

Oliver, Frederick S., *Alexander Hamilton* (London, 1906).

Parton, James, *Life of Aaron Burr* (Boston, 1885, 2 vols.).

———, *Life of Thomas Jefferson* (Boston, 1884).

Randall, Henry S., *Life of Thomas Jefferson* (New York, 1858, 3 vols.).

Russell, Phillips, *Benjamin Franklin, the First Civilized American* (New York, 1926).

Schachner, Nathan, *Alexander Hamilton* (New York, 1957).

Sparks, Jared, *Life of Gouverneur Morris with Selections from His Correspondence and Miscellaneous Papers* (Boston, 1832, 3 vols.).

Swiggett, Howard, *The Extraordinary Mr. Morris* (Garden City, 1952).

Van Doren, Carl, *Benjamin Franklin* (New York, 1938).

Wharton, Anne H., *Martha Washington* (New York, 1897).

GENERAL HISTORIES AND SPECIAL STUDIES

Abernethy, Thomas P., *Western Lands and the American Revolution* (New York, 1937).

————, *The Burr Conspiracy* (New York, 1954).

Alvord, Clarence W., *The Mississippi Valley in British Politics* (Cleveland, 1917, 2 vols.).

Beard, Charles A., *Economic Interpretation of the Constitution* (New York, 1913).

————, *Economic Origens of Jeffersonian Democracy* (New York, 1915).

Becker, Carl L., *The Declaration of Independence* (New York, 1940).

Bemis, Samuel F., *The Diplomacy of the American Revolution* (New York, 1935).

————, *Jay's Treaty* (New York, 1923).

Bowers, Claude G., *Jefferson and Hamilton* (New York, 1925).

Bullock, Helen D., *My Head and My Heart* (New York, 1945).

Channing, Edward, *History of the United States* (New York, 1917, 4 vols.).

Dauer, Manning J., *The Adams Federalists* (Baltimore, 1935).

Hamilton, John C., *History of the Republic of the United States* (New York, 1857-1864, 7 vols.).

Hendrick, Burton J., *The Lees of Virginia* (Boston, 1935).

Hofstadter, Richard, *The American Political Tradition and the Men Who Made It* (New York, 1949).

Kurtz, Stephen G., *The Presidency of John Adams* (Philadelphia, 1957).

Link, Eugene P., *Democratic-Republican Societies, 1790-1800* (New York, 1942).

Livingston, Edwin B., *The Livingstons of Livingston Manor* (New York, 1910).

Parrington, Vernon L., *Main Currents in American Thought* (New York, 1926, 3 vols.).

Van Doren, Carl, *The Secret History of the American Revolution* (New York, 1941).

ARTICLES

Gallacher, S. A., "Franklin's Way to Wealth," *Journal of English and Germanic Philology*, XLVIII (18), 220-251.

Larson, Harold, "Alexander Hamilton: The Fact and the Fiction of His Early Years," *William and Mary Quarterly,* IX (3rd series), 139-151.

Lyon, E. Wilson, "The Franco-American Convention of 1800," *Journal of Modern History,* XII (1940), 305-333.

Marsh, Philip, "Hamilton and Monroe," *Mississippi Valley Historical Review,* XXXIV, 459-469.

Index